DIFFERENT WAYS TO SUPPORT THE RURAL POOR

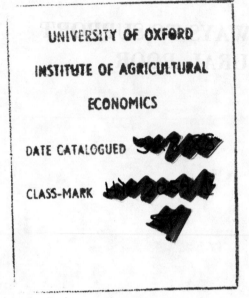

DIFFERENT WAYS TO SUPPORT THE RURAL POOR

Effects of Two Development Approaches in Bangladesh

Pieter Streefland
Hasina Ahmed
Marium Nafisa
Dalem Ch. Barman
H. K. Arefeen

Distributed by
The Centre for Social Studies
Room No. 1107, Arts Building
Dhaka University
Dhaka-2, Bangladesh

Also distributed by
The Royal Tropical Institute
63 Mauritskade
1092 AD Amsterdam, The Netherlands

ISBN 90 6832 015 7

Cover design
A. Rahman

Printed by
Kazi Mukul
Dana Printers Ltd.
Ga-16 Mohakhali, Dhaka-12.
Phone : 602019

The research for this publication was financed by the Netherlands Minister for Development Cooperation, who also shares copyright. Citation is encouraged. Short excerpts may be translated and/or reproduced without prior permission, on the condition that the source is indicated. For translation and/or reproduction in whole the Section for Research and Technology of the aforementioned Minister (P.O. BOX 20061, 2500 EB The Hague) should be notified in advance. Responsibility for the contents and for the opinions expressed rests solely with the authors ; publication does not constitute an endorsement by the Netherlands Minister for Development Cooperation.
Dhaka, September 1986

Dhaka, September 1986

Contents

LIST OF TABLES

LIST OF CASES

LIST OF MAPS

Preface

This book is the final report of a study of medium term effects of two development approaches, one emphasizing material support, the other non-material support. Both development approaches have the same general objective : to alleviate rural poverty by supporting the rural poor. This objective is realized by way of development projects : we have surveyed the results of two of such projects, one in Sunamganj District, the other in Tangail District. In each case fieldwork took six months.

Readers should note that our study, though it focussed on two different development approaches, is not meant to be a comparative study. Each of the development approaches is important in its own way and should be appreciated as such. Consequently, there is a separate chapter on each of them, which may be read separately.

The study could only be realized because of support received from various sides. We would, first, like to thank the Dutch Minister of Development Cooperation for financing the study. We also thank Prof. B.K. Jahangir and his colleagues at the Centre for Social Studies, Dhaka University for providing the necessary logistic support. Further, we want to thank Mr. F. H. Abed of BRAC and Prof. M. Yunus of Grameen Bank, as well as the officials at the headquarters and local offices of these organizations, for their cooperation and support. Finally, we express our deep gratitude to the poor villagers who put up with us for six months, and shared with us their views and experiences. We dedicate our study to them.

Dhaka, September 1986.

Chapter I : Introduction

1. The Rural Poverty Situation

Though they differ in perspective and methodology, the conclusion of studies on rural society in Bangladesh is usually more or less the same ; there is an immense and increasing degree of poverty. Looking at various poverty indicators, the following picture emerges. In the field of nutrition there are consistently low levels of nutrient intakes (Hassan and Ahmed, 1984). The health situation is characterized by prominence of poverty related diseases. Besides, government health care facilities and services have been found to operate badly in the countryside (Akhter et al., 1981 ; Ashraf et al., 1982). The literacy level is low, especially among women, and does not show real improvement in recent years (Hossain et al., 1986 ; Grant, 1985). Real wages of agricultural labourers, an important category in the countryside, have deteriorated, while relations between labourers and land-owners have lost most of their protective elements (Arefeen, 1986 ; Hartman and Boyce 1983 ; Khan, 1977, 1984 ; van Schendel, 1981 ; van Schendel and Faraizi, 1984). For those who have little or no access to agricultural land, the most important means of production in the rural areas, there are, as yet, very few possibilities for work outside agriculture. Mostly, they work under appalling conditions at brick kilns, road works or, in case of men, as rickshawpullers in the towns. Occasionally, they are able to engage in petty trading.

2. Efforts to Alleviate Rural Poverty

After the War of Liberation (1971) aid from abroad started pouring in. Initially, most of it was geared towards relief and reconstruction, but in course of time external assistance became more directed at technical support, particularly in order to increase agricultural production and productivity. Food aid was (and is) an important addition. Other fields which received considerable support were health care and family planning.

The Bangladesh economy still leans rather heavily on foreign assistance (Sobhan, 1982). Much of the external support is intended to alleviate the rural poverty conditions described above. It seems, however, that in general, governmental efforts to alleviate rural poverty do not really benefit those for whom they are meant (BRAC, 1980 ; Hartman and Boyce, 1983 ; de Vylder, 1982). Foreign aid which is channelled via non-government development organizations (NGDOs) appears to have a better record in that respect (Ahmed, 1980 a and b).

Initially the aid efforts of NGDOs were also characterized by their relief character. In a few years' time, however, community development and rural health care efforts and projects aiming at an increase of agricultural production emerged, signifying thematic differentiation in non-government rural development policy.

Taking a closer look at recent history, we can observe that some NGDOs, e.g. BRAC (Bangladesh Rural Advancement Committee) and GK (Gono Shasthaya Kendra), show a rather impressive policy development (Ahmed, 1980 a and b). From the second half of the 1970s, their projects, as well as the more recent ones of new NGDOs, like Nijera Kori and ASA (Association for Social Advancement) are characterized by a clear delineation of target-categories among the rural population. Further, by the formation of groups as recipients of support. This organizational orientation came about in order to have better ways of reaching wider goals, such as improving the health status of the poor, but also as a goal in itself, in the sense of strengthening the weak by increasing their unity. In addition, a tendency can generally be observed to put more emphasis on activities directed at enhancing the target-group's understanding of the background of its poverty and backward situation, and at promoting its confidence in possibilities to change its condition by concerted action. In projects which are extreme examples of this development approach, material support may not be provided at all.

Another policy direction which is followed by NGDOs is an emphasis on providing the poor with material support, particularly in the form of credit. In this way they would be able to strengthen their economic basis. Sometimes this policy includes the formation of groups as well. A well known NGDO which has already done much work in this respect is Grameen Bank.*

* Grameen Bank presently is a scheduled bank It comes

Though there is a multitude of evaluation reports, very little is, in fact, known about the longer term effects of the different development approaches which characterize projects and programmes of NGDOs. Here, we define a development approach as the combination of a problemanalysis, the formulation of a solution to the problem, and the specific interventions based on both. The present study is an effort to contribute to filling this gap in our knowledge and, as such, to provide building stones for an even sounder basis to the work of NGDOs concerned with the rural poor.

3. The Analytical Framework

With regard to the considerable differentiation among development approaches, a study which contrasts the longer term effects of a few of them would seem to be potentially most fruitful. In this way it would be possible to discern strengths and weaknesses of different approaches. After due consideration and consultations with a large number of NGDOs in Bangladesh it was decided to direct the attention at two types of approaches : those which put most emphasis on material support of the target-group (especially by supplying credit) and those which put most emphasis on awareness rising.

The above formulation reflects that we are, in reality, not always dealing with clearcut distinctions between development approaches. In one project, elements of different

under the Ministry of Finances and does not operate under the Banking Act. For all purpose it makes its own policy. Hence, we may consider it as an NGDO.

approaches may be represented, with one approach being more or less predominant. The best way to study the two development approaches we are concerned with here, is to envisage a continuum, with at one extreme an approach heavily emphasizing supply of credit and at the other end one which stresses conscientization. In the middle of this continuum one would find a mixed approach.

All positions on the continuum would, of course, be ideal types. The next step to take is to relate these idealtypes to reality by searching for projects which are characterized by development approaches more or less resembling the extremes of the continuum. Provided these projects have been going on for a reasonable period–in this case we choose a period of at least five years–a study of their material and immaterial, positive and negative consequences for the rural poor would provide us with insight in the effects of approaches we have been looking for.

The present study focuses on the position of the rural poor as the dependent variable. Regarding this position an analytical distinction has been made between four different, reciprocally influencing, aspects. Consequently. these aspects have been operationalized by selecting indicators in order to direct the collection of data. The following aspects were studied :

(i) The *economic* aspect, to be defined as the level at which a household is able to economically provide for itself. Some selected indicators are : sources of income of the household, quantity and quality of the food being consumed : its level of indebtedness ; ownership of utensils, cattle and agricultural tools, condition of its living quarters. With regard to the position of women their economic dependency within the household is gauged, as well as their leeway to decide on the spending of household funds ;

(ii) the *political* aspect : at village and regional levels this implies the level of bargaining power of the rural poor (both men and women) with regard to the rural elite and to the government administration. Moreover, the degree to which the poor are politically independent as to whom to support at elections. At the household level it concerns, first, the relative power that husband and wife (adult men and women) have with regard to economic decisions and decisions regarding marriage and education of their children Second, it concerns the degree to and ways in which the husband tries to prevent his wife from increa sing, her scope to move around and m eet others. Finally it concerns the general treatment of women in the house.

Some of the selected indicators in this regard are the voting behaviour of the poor, the quality of labour relations and the way in which the poor are treated by the rural elite in everyday life. Moreover, the nature of decision making within the household and the prevalence of divorces and wife-beating will be examined :

(iii) the *organizational* aspect, to be defined as : to what extent and in which ways have the rural poor become organized on the basis of their being poor i.e. on a class basis. Obviously, this can be studied on village as well as supravillage level. Indicators are : the nature and continuity of the groups which have been organized in the context of the project, the characteristics of leadership and mutual assistance and collective action among the poor ;

(iv) the *subjective* aspect regards the level of confidence which the poor have in possibilities to improve their situation by their own activities and in cooperation with others in the same position. At the level of behaviour we may study this by looking at collective action and organization.* At the level of meaning, it is studied by looking at people's orientation with regard to their present and their future, i.e. at their world view. In order to do this in a more systematic way, we shall gauge their views by comparing them with (elements of) two ideal types of orientations, the survival model and the emancipation model (Figure I). Of course, these models are theoretical constructs, points of reference to guide us when studying this difficult matter. But after the fieldwork it is possible to describe the world view of the poor more realistically.

---

* In fact, we may consider the subjective aspect as the cognitive side of the organizational aspect as it is defined above.

Figure 1. Worldviews of the Rural Poor

Survival Model	*Emancipation Model*
i. a tendency to strive for security ;	i. a tendency to strive for improvement of one's economic position ;
ii. a conviction that a supreme being, or fate, or an iron law of destiny fixes one's position in life ;	ii. a conviction that actions of other people determine one's position in life to a considerable extent ;
iii. a tendency to look for external support (patrons, relief organizations) ;	iii. confidence in the possibility to change one's situation by one's own actions;
iv. The household, the village, the kin group are principal points of reference ;	iv. recognition of the fact that one's socio-economic position is shared with others ;
v. Cooperation with others primarily takes place in the context of these reference points.	v. recognition of the need to cooperate with others in the same position to reach the goal of improvement of one's socio-economic situation.

4. The Methodology

The team and the time schedule

The study was initiated by the research advisor Dr. Pieter A. Streefland of the Royal Tropical Institute in Amsterdam, the Netherlands, who has been working intermittently in Bangladesh and other parts of South Asia for the last fifteen years. With financial support of the Netherlands Ministry of Development Cooperation he made an arrangement with Professor B. K. Jahangir of the Centre for Social Studies, University of Dhaka, to carry out the study jointly, The Centre fielded a four member team consisting of two highly experienced male researchers, Dr. H. K. Arefeen (team leader) and Dr. Dalem Ch. Barman and two female researchers, Miss. Hasina Ahmed and Miss. Marium Nafisa, who combined a high level of motivation with a considerable degree of research insight and experience.

During the fieldwork the team was split up into two subteams ; the remaining activities were carried out by the whole team. Each of the sub-teams, consisting of a male and a female researcher, collected research data at one of the locations. One sub-team, working in a Hindu-majority area was able to carry out the fieldwork jointly ; the members of the other sub-team worked separately, with the female researcher concentrating on the women and her male colleague on the men. Information on fieldwork problems can be found in the Methodological Note (Annexure II).

The actual study began in October 1985. During an introductory period the team and the research advisor held extensive meetings in Dhaka on matters of methodology and logistics, took decisions on locations and definitions, and prepared research tools. Next, during November and December the two sub-teams were in the field, familiarizing with locations and respondents and conducting a census. During this first fieldwork phase, the researchers also collected information about history and ecology of villages and their region, and about the project activities of which they would study the effects.

In January 1986 the team processed the census data and discussed the results with the research advisor at Dhaka. Further, samples were drawn and interview checklists prepared, always after thorough discussions. Besides, a start was made, with the ground-work needed for the forthcoming analysis of data. Finally, research problems, both experienced and foreseen were, dealt with.

Consequently, the team again went into the field, for two stints of about two months, interrupted by a break in Dhaka. Conducting in-depth interviews with men and women in the sample households was the core activity. Besides, they continued to extend their insight in the dynamics of village society and in the particulars of past and present project intervention. For these purposes they interviewed key informants and conducted group interviews. To standardize the collection of data on general matters, the team had composed detailed checklists on village, region and projects during their earlier Dhaka stays.

In July, the research advisor returned to Bangladesh. Discussions were held on the results of the work done, and a framework for the analysis of data and for the report to be written on the basis of this was set up. Next, a period of analysis, reflection and writing followed, which in September 1986 resulted in the present report.

Making choices

The villages

As was set forth at the beginning of the chapter, the study aimed at contrasting longer term effects of certain approaches characteristic of projects designed to improve the situation of the rural poor. An important task was, of course, the selection of these projects. After studying the relevant NGDO activities as they had developed after the War of Liberation-partly for this purpose the research advisor, already quite familiar with the world of NGDOs, paid two visits to Bangladesh in 1984–it was decided to select a project in Sunamganj and one in Tangail.

Consequently, in consultation with the respective NGDOs within both projects areas villages were selected where the field work was to take place. Moreover, as we wanted to gauge effects of the influence of the project interventions, and as sufficient baseline data were lacking, it was necessary to also select two control villages in the immediate vicinity of the project villages. Assuming that effects of ecological changes, administrative measures and other development interventions would be approximately the same in a village and its control, differences found between the situation of the poor in both villages could with reasonable confidence be attributed to the interventions we were interested in (Figure II).

Figure II. Schematic view of research situation

		interventions	
study village	A	↓ ↓ ↓ ↓	A1
situation at the time of introduction of intervention			situation at the time of the study
control village	B	— — — — — —	B1

Note: as no sufficient data are available about stuation A, the effects of interventions have to be studied by comparing Al with Bl.

For the ultimate selection two factors were decisive. First, the project must have been as effective as possible in the villages concerned. In other words the, interventions must have been administered as they were supposed to. As it was not feasible to do a pre-evaluation on this point, we took the advices of the NGDOs concerned as to in which villages they considered their project to have been carried out successfully. Second, near the eligible project village there should be another one where no interventions by the specific project had been carried out. Though not without difficulty, four villages were found. They will be described in the following chapters. Both sub-teams succeeded in finding lodgings near to the villages to be studied.

Delineating the rural poor

Though both the study projects were aiming at improving the situation of the rural poor, their definitions of this target-group were slightly dissimilar. Besides, neither gave insight in the stratification of the village as a whole, information which is essential for a study which contrasts various villages. We developed our own definition, based on a wider picture of village society and also easy to use as a research tool. Next, we chose to avoid the tricky and extremely labour intensive path of taking access to land, or income, as a basic indicator. Instead, we selected another approach, which had twice been tried out before and, to our knowledge, rather successfully (Ashraf et al, 1982 ; van Schendel, 1981). This approach took the household as point of departure. It established a ranking of households in the village by economic categories. Each of the categories was defined in terms of the extent to which a household had been able to provide for itself during the previous agricultural year (April 1984-April 1985). A household was defined as a residential unit composed of one or more individuals living together and eating food from the same kitchen, including those presently absent for less than 15 days and including guests who have been staying for more than 15 days. In line with the studies already mentioned, during the census all households in the four villages were assigned to one of four economic categories. When in doubt about precision or reliability of the information provided, the researchers also took data on sources of income, housing conditions and ownership of cattle, implements and utensils into account. The categories used were :

a, households unable to provide for themselves for the

full twelve months at a very low standard of living ;

b. households just able to provide for themselves at a very low standard of living ;

c. households able to provide for themselves at a moderate standard of living, even from one to three months in excess of the year ;

d. households able to provide for themselves at a comfortable standard of living and for more than three months in excess.

We chose to consider households in categories A and B as the rural poor. Obviously, the economic categories used are rather wide. Theoretically, many more categories could be designed, though it depends on the composition of a specific village society, and on the skewdness of its stratification, if and to what degree each category will be filled. Moreover, it is important to realise that each categorization is, in fact, only a snapshot of a village society which is changing continuously.

Due to constraints of time and manpower it was not feasible to conduct in-depth interviews with adult men and women in each of the village households during the second field—work phase. Samples had to be drawn. The census data supplied a clear basic picture of the composition of villages and households. For each village we knew how many households fell in each of the four initial categories. Besides, we had information on the age and sex composition of each household, as well as on the status of their participation in the projects studied. In both the project villages we found that categories A and B contained sufficient households where nobody had participated in project activities to enable us to also choose an intra-village control group. Though availability of an internal control group could be considered as a bonus, comparative use of data collected from households included in it, ought to be done carefully. It would be necessary to check on the possibility of selective bias in this respect, as non-participation might be related to factors pertaining to the subject of the study.

Samples were drawn according to the following principles. First, households of categories A, B and C would be included in the village samples. Second, if possible, all households in one village and one category would be included in the sample. Third, if the number of households in a certain category and village would be considered too large, the procedure would be to, first, draw a random sample of households participating in project activities and, next, to draw a control sample from among the remaining households, in that village and category. Another control sample of approximately the same size would be drawn from the same category in the respective control village. The control samples were initially drawn at random. After trying to match each of the selected households on the basis of sex and age composition with a household in the initial sample of project households, sometimes necessary adjustments were made in the control samples. Lists were drawn up of the matching pattern between specific households, to be used later during the analysis of the interview information.

In the project village in Sunamganj the procedure was more complicated. This village was by far the most sizeable of the four. Moreover it consisted of two geographically distinct parts and had a population of mixed religious composition. In this case we, first, took a cluster sample and selected the western part of the village, as in this part the project had been most influential. Second, we stratified the other samples on the basis of religious background of households. Muslim and Hindu households being included with a ratio of 4 : 3, which corresponds with the religious composition of the whole village.

The six samples which were the result of our sampling procedure will be referred to as follows. The Sunamganj samples as S^1 and S^2 (controls) for the project village and S^3 for the control village. The Tangail samples as T^1 and T^2 (controls) for the project village and T^3 for the control village. For the composition of the samples see Table 1. 1.

Table 1.1 : Composition and size of samples of households in the study villages.

Sunamganj Project Village

Category	Number of households (cluster)	
	Total	Sample
A	146	50 (25 controls)
B	23	8 (4 controls)
C	3	3
D	2	0
Total	174	61

Sunamganj Control Village

Category	Number of households	
	Total	Sample
A	66	17
B	24	10
C	8	3
D	9	0
Total	107	30

Tangail Project Village

Category	Number of households	
	Total	Sample
A	20	20 (10 controls)
B	35	24 (10 controls)
C	12	8 (4 controls)
D	5	0
Total	72	52

Tangail Control Village

Category	Number of households	
	Total	Samples
A	48	12
B	39	10
C	26	5
D	10	0
Total	123	27

MAP NO. 1

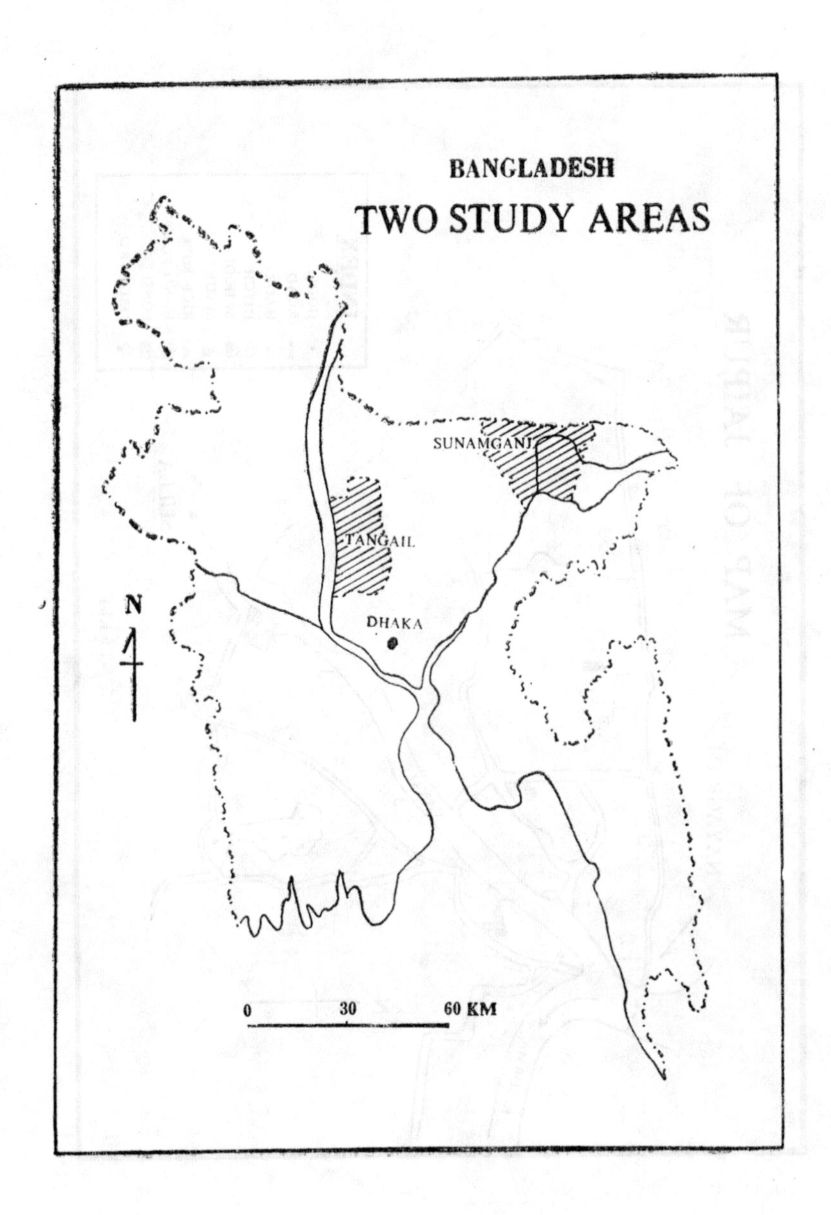
BANGLADESH
TWO STUDY AREAS
SUNAMGANJ
TANGAIL
DHAKA
N
0
30
60 KM

MAP NO. 2

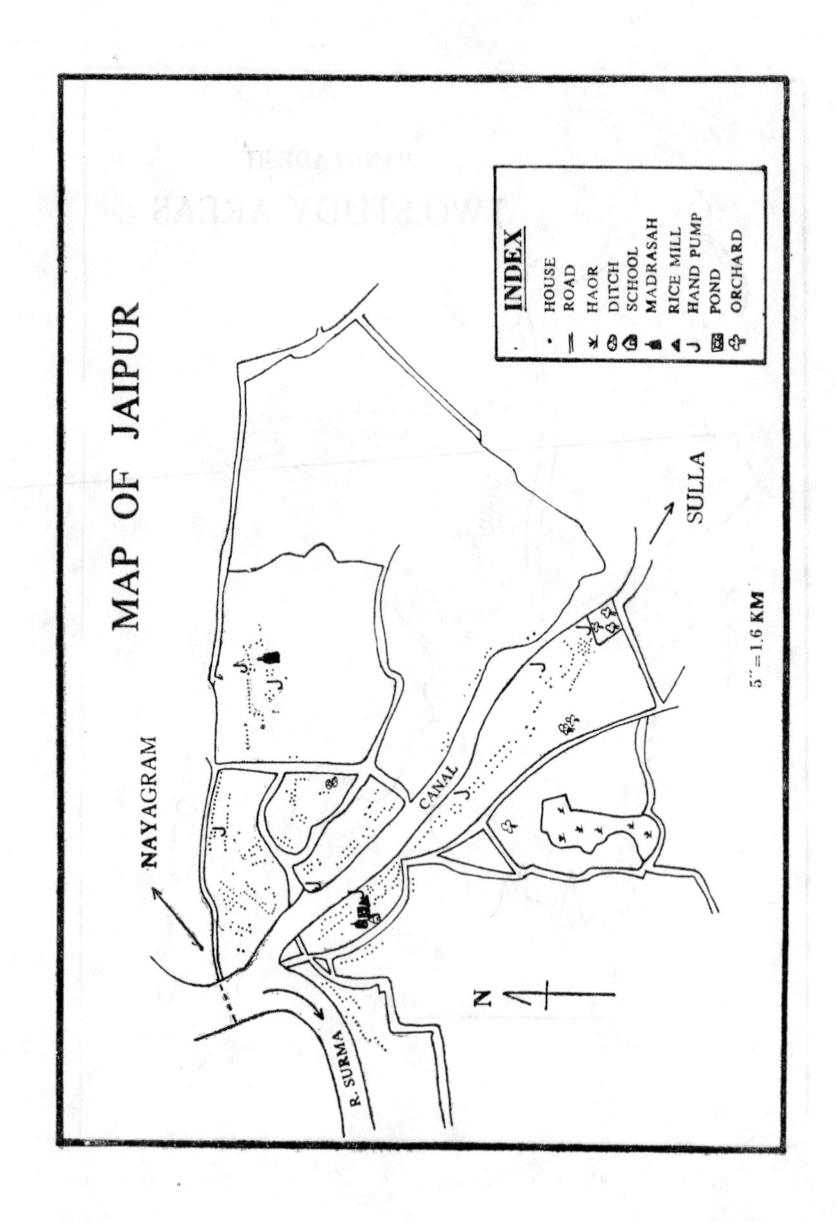
MAP OF JAIPUR
INDEX
HOUSE
ROAD
HAOR
DITCH
SCHOOL
MADRASAH
RICE MILL
HAND PUMP
POND
ORCHARD
NAYAGRAM
SULLA
CANAL
R. SURMA
N
5" = 1.6 KM

MAP NO. 3

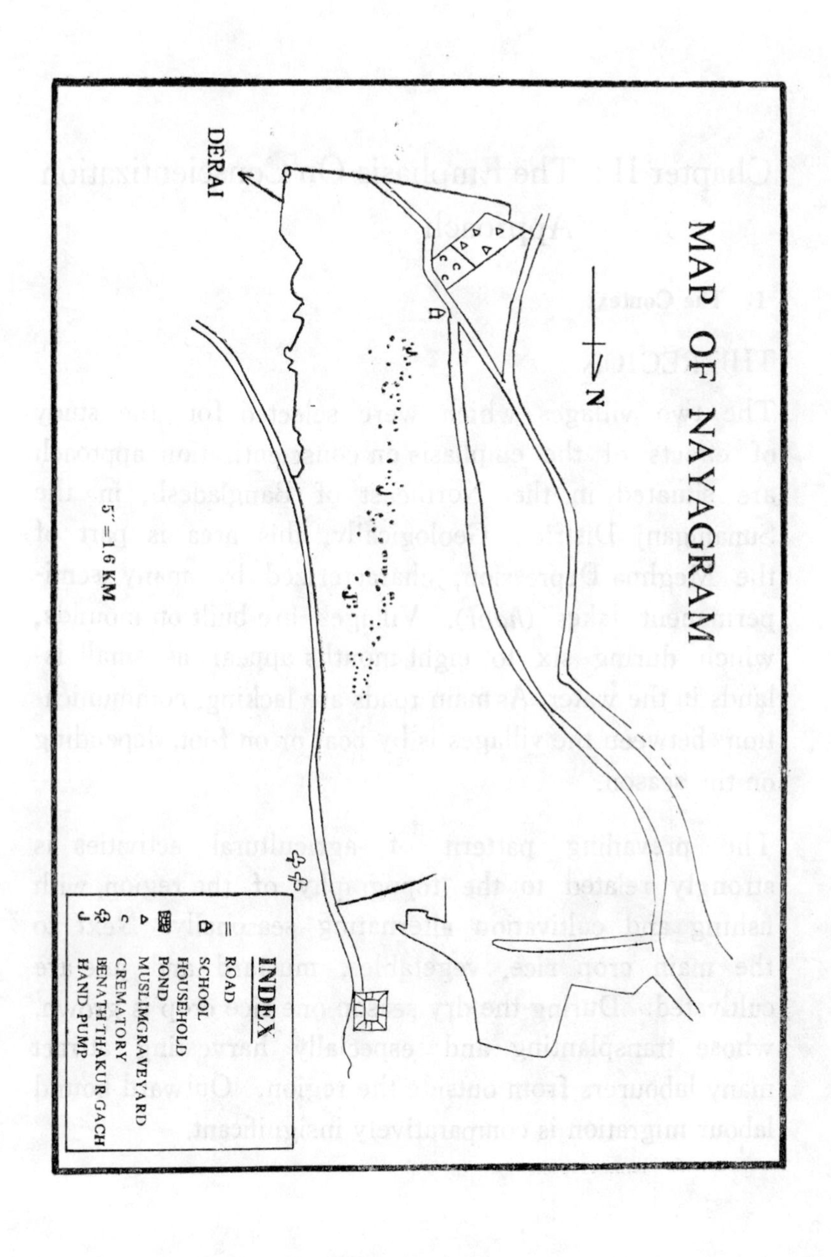
MAP OF NAYAGRAM
N
DERAI
5" = 1.6 KM
INDEX
ROAD
SCHOOL
HOUSEHOLD
POND
MUSLIMGRAVEYARD
CREMATORY
BENATH THAKUR GACH
HAND PUMP

Chapter II : The Emphasis On Conscientization Approach

1. The Context

THE REGION

The two villages which were selected for the study of effects of the emphasis on conscientization approach are situated in the Northeast of Bangladesh, in the Sunamganj District. Geologically, this area is part of the Meghna Depression, characterized by many semi-permanent lakes (*haor*). Villages are built on mounds, which during six to eight months appear as small islands in the water. As main roads are lacking, communication between the villages is by boat or on foot, depending on the season.

The prevailing pattern of agricultural activities is strongly related to the topography of the region, with fishing and cultivation alternating seasonally. Next to the main crop rice, vegetables, mustard and jute are cultivated. During the dry season one rice crop is grown, whose transplanting and especially harvesting attract many labourers from outside the region. Outward bound labour migration is comparatively insignificant.

In the towns industrial activities are restricted to small-scale industries, such as rice mills and pump repair workshops. Presently, there are indications that in Derai town, which is quite near to both villages, industrial growth is picking up since its upgrading to *Upazila* headquarters.

Since long both Hindus and Muslims have inhabited the region, though their proportions have changed in 1947 and, again, in 1971. Apart from incidents in these marked years, coexistence of both groups appears to be rather peaceful. In the administration we observed a predominance of Muslims in appointed positions and Hindus in elected posts.

THE VILLAGES

The Project Village

General

Jaipur belongs to Sulla *Upazila* and is partly situated on the bank of the river Surma, which flows through both Sulla and Derai *Upazila.* A canal divides the village into an eastern and a western part. The *Upazila* headquarters are situated nearby. Daily and bi-weekly markets are held there, as well as in the nearby village Sarma.

Population

Jaipur is a large village, with a total population of 2205, distributed over 421 households. Among these, 310 households (73.6%) are Muslim and the remaining 111 belong to the Hindu community. At the time of the census, there were 1094 men and 1111 women in the village, which corresponds with a male/female ratio of 98. Under fifteens form 44.4% of the village population.

Of the two geographical parts of the village, the eastern side comprises 247, all Muslim, households, while the western side is inhabited by 174 households, 63 of which are Muslim and 111 Hindu. Because of its mixed religious composition, its smaller size and a relatively high degree of project implementation, it was decided to select the western side as a cluster to take the more specific household sample form. In the western part the male/female ratio is 99. While under fifteens form 41.3% of the population.

As to the educational level we found that in the whole village 81.0% of the heads of households and 91.3% of all women over 15 years of age had not received any formal education.* In the western part of the village these percentages were, respectively, 74.7 and 85.7.

With respect to the economic categorization of the village population, as defined in the introductory chapter. We can see the distribution in Table 2.1. Both in the village as a whole and in its western part we observe a predominance of A category households and people, which marks Jaipur as a really poor village.

Within the two religious communities there are vari-

---

* formal education refers to attendance of a regular primary or secondary school. It does not refer to *madrasa* education which we indicate as informal education.

ous subgroups. Among the Muslims there are those who have lived since long in the village and the settlers, who have come from the former Mymensingh District. Among the original Muslims there are two distinct communities with a professional background, the Nagarsi (Drum beaters) and the Chor, who are traditionally professional thieves. Though the different Muslim groups do not intermarry, they participate in the same village meetings, for instance at the occasion of *Eid.*

Among the Hindus there are six subcaste communities : Das, Biswas, Sukla Baidya, Roy, Barber and Blacksmith. Though the subcastes organize social activities separately, also at supra-village level, they also celebrate some festivals together. All Hindus belong to the original inhabitants of the village. Among them the Das and Biswas communities are by far the largest.

Agricultural

The main rice crop is transplanted *boro,* which is sown in October/November and harvested in May/June. Another important rice crop is transplanted Irri, introduced at the end of the 1960s, which is transplanted at the same time as the *boro* but can be harvested a month earlier. Mustard, potatoes and vegetables are grown from October till March/April. Their cultivation has been introduced and/or boosted by the Project since 1972.

The agricultural year 1984/85 was an average one, but then, in early 1986, disaster struck in the form

Table 2. 1 : Economic categorization of households and people in Jaipur and Nayagram

	Jaipur				Jaipur-West				Nayagram			
	No.	%	No	%	No	%	No	%	No	%	No	%
A	356	84.6	1691	76.9	146	83.9	694	73.4	66	61.7	253	42.6
B	52	12.4	328	14.9	23	13.2	161	17.0	24	22.4	152	25.6
C	7	1.7	88	4.0	3	1.7	49	5.2	8	7.5	72	12.1
D	6	1.4	98	4.4	2	1.2	42	4.4	9	8.4	117	19.7
Total	421	100.1	2205	100.2	174	100.0	946	100.0	107	100.0	594	100.0

Source : Census November-December 1985

of hailstorms, heavily damaging both the practically ripe Irri and the ripening *boro* crops. All who are involved in agriculture suffered losses. The poor in the forms of work and payment for services already rendered. For them the only bright spot was that the owners did not take much action to get in the crop and allowed gleaning of the damaged crop.

Land and labour

Besides ownerships, a form of tenancy prevails which is locally called *rangjama*. It is a one year contract, which includes pre-payment of an amount of money against the use of the land. The owner has no claim on any products, but also no liability for damages to the crop. Next, there is sharecropping (*borga*) which includes a fifty/fifty sharing of the crop, with the sharecropper providing all the inputs. Mortgage is insignificant in the area.

Agricultural labour comes in different forms. When working on a daily basis, local labourers usually are paid in cash, with three meals in addition to that. But many of them hire themselves out on an eight months' contract, which may include also other than agricultural activities. Quite often the contract labourers stay far off in the field to till the land or protect the standing crop, sleeping in makeshift shelters. Such eight months' contracts include payment in kind at the end, though an advance may be given against interest. Moreover, clothes, board and lodging are supplied. Migrant labourers, who during the harvest may number ten times the local workforce, are always paid in kind for cutting the crop. Their contracts are arranged well in advance by middlemen, who usually bind the landowners by providing loans. Migrants who come for transplanting are less in number, have a slightly different geographical background and are paid on a day to day basis.

Then there is the provision of *khas* land. This is government owned land, which is de facto often used by the village elite for grazing or cultivation, but which may, according to the law, be given out on lease to landless villagers. As we shall see below, access to *khas* land has been both a source of intra-village conflict and a major issue in the process of emancipation of the local poor.

Due to the extensive damage of the standing crops in early 1986 the above picture does not properly reflect the reality of the agricultural year 1985/86. Virtually everyone involved in agriculture faced severe losses. There was less work for labourers and those on an eight months' contract might find their employer unable to pay them off. Owner-cultivators, ***borgadar*** and those who advanced money on a ***rangjama*** tenancy contract faced a major disaster. Fewer migrant labourers came at harvest time, but those who did asked for a larger part of the crop they managed to cut.

Village politics

Before the Liberation War local-level politics were clearly a matter of the two religious communities separately, with the Muslim having better access to government resources. The prominent Muslim leader was Mr. Anwar, a landowner whose brother-in-law was chairman of the local Union Committee and whose position as *imam* of the mosque in an adjacent village gave him prestige and influence. Among the Hindus two leader stood out, one from the Das and one from the Biswas community.

During the War, the Muslims of Jaipur sided with Pakistan. Many of them enrolled as trustees to fight the pro-liberation forces. The local Hindus left for India, to return in 1972. After the War, many of those who had been on Pakistan's side were killed. Mr. Anwar was only just able to save his life. He then had to face a situation where a national NGDO began a large scale relief operation in region and village, especially among the, most affected, Hindu population.

In late 1972 the NGDO changed the focus of its activities from relief to development. In due course this led to the emergence of the leadership of Mrs. Hasina. She received support from the NGDO in the form of training and played a leading role in project activities. Her following consisted of many of the local poor and of some better-off women, among whom Mr. Anwar's cousin (mo. si. da). So, since the War a pattern of two major factions arose. One faction centred around Mr. Anwar and consisted of local Muslims from different economic categories, poor as well as rich. The other converged on Mrs. Hasina and consisted of Muslim participants in development activities of the NGDO and members of the Hindu Biswas community. A bit later, this faction also got the support of a young local Muslim lawyer, Mr. Ramiz. His interest in supporting Mrs. Hasina was dual : a joint alignment against his enemy Mr. Anwar and a possibility to recruit members for a left-wing political party. Two local communities, the Chor and the Das, do not have a permanent alignment but try to choose sides in time of need (the Chor) or to keep neutral (the Das).

Politics in Jaipur cannot just be characterized as factionalism. It also contains strong elements of opposed class interests. This became clear during a period of conflict about access to *khas* land in the early 1980s. Both factions suffered heavy losses and none emerged as the sole winner. Mr. Anwar's position was weakened, as the conflict costs included sale of land and loss of prestige. Moreover, for other reasons, he lost his *imamship* and the support of a strong ally in a neighbouring village. Mrs. Hasina gained stature as a leader, also outside the village. She and her followers could not, however, establish permanent access to the *khas* land. They controlled it only for one season and presently the other faction has de facto control over the land As we shall see later, a Project group which had been formed by local poor men dissolved in the wake of the conflict. Besides, already at an earlier stage about a quarter of its members changed sides to Mr. Anwar.

Development activities

Apart from scattered Food for Work activities and

possibilities to get loans through the Bangladesh Rural Development Board (BRDB) and the Krishi Bank, development work with direct relevance to the poor in Jaipur has been dominated by the aforementioned NGDO. Henceforth, we shall refer to this development work as the Project : it is discussed later in a separate section.

The Control Village

General

Nayagram is situated in Derai *Upazila* at a distance of nearly three kilometers from the project village. Except for the southern side, where it borders on two other villages, Nayagram is surrounded by *bil* (extremely low lying area) and fallow land (see map 3). Each year floods strike heavily at Nayagram's land, taking away some of the fertile topsoil. Though it was included in the relief programme, the village has not remained under coverage of the Project in its later stages. Probably it was not included in the community development phase in 1972 because it was perceived at the time as having low accessibility and development potential, criteria which were used to redefine the total coverage area when the relief phase was concluded.

Population

Nayagram is a small village, certainly compared to Jaipur, with a total population of 594, distributed over 107 households. All inhabitants are Hindus, who belong to the Das community. There is a section of immigrants from two nearby villages which were deserted due to heavy floods about thirty years ago

We counted 303 men and 291 women in the village, i. e. a male/female ratio of 104. The percentage of under fifteens was 37.9. As regards the educational level, the following picture emerged : 62.3% of the heads of households and 64.1% of the women over fifteen had not received any formal education. The difference between these figures and those, pertaining to Jaipur must be attributed to the Hindu background of Nayagram. This implies more emphasis on formal education, as compared to an interest in *madrasa* education, and more possibilities for girls to attend school.

The economic categorization of the village population is presented in Table 2.1. Though A category households and people clearly dominate, they do so considerably less than in Jaipur. In other words, Nayagram is less poor than the project village.

Agriculture, land and labour

What was stated about Jaipur in these respects also applies here, with three exceptions. One is the larger erosive impact of the floods, which was already mentioned. The second is the presence of a powertiller in the village, which is rented by the owner to others, and whose engine is also used for ricemilling. The third is the absence of a *khas* land issue. The Nayagram *khas* land lies fallow and is used for grazing by those who own cattle (see also Case no. 7).

Village politics

Since the 1983 elections there have been two factions in

Nayagram, Before that time important political decisions were made on a subcaste basis, Das people from three adjoining villages taking part in the decision-making. The core leaders of both factions are comparatively well-to-do, well-educated and well-connected men. Neither the difference between settlers and original inhabitants, nor that between rich and poor has played a role in the way the factions have split the population.

Development activities

No national or international NGDO has initiated development work in Nayagram. Since about four years there have been two male and one female BRDB cooperative societies in the village. The female group is presently dormant; the male group include some poor and mostly better-off villagers among their members. About three years ago eight men independently formed a credit cooperative.

THE PROJECT

Since its inception in 1972 the Project went through various stages, each characterized by a special configuration of activities, emphasis in approach, and a concomitant organizational setup. From late 1976 onwards, a clear and consistent pattern has emerged consisting of emphasis on conscientization and organization building of poor men and women. This was increasingly accompanied by a withdrawal of Project staff.

This, is of course, not the place to describe and analyze the changes the Project went through in any depth.

It suffices to sum up their general features. The changes which came about were, however, linked to certain background factors. Some of these deserve to be briefly mentioned here. The experiences in the field, including the contact of staff with the poor and their conditions of poverty were a major factor. It was combined with a continuous and at its peaks sometimes conflictuous exchange of ideas among the staff. Part of them had originally been recruited locally. They were often less educated and articulate than those staff members who came from elsewhere in the country, bringing along ideas on how to eradicate rural poverty. So, discussions and social dynamics have been important forces for change from within the Project, of course, besides other factors. With this remark we shall leave the subject of Project staff. It only remains to be pointed out that there is good reason to assume that those staff who have been working in Jaipur were for the Project average quality or above.

The Project started as a relief operation in three *thana* of the then Sylhet District, covering more than 200 villages. In this Hindu-majority region the effects of the War had been devastating. The Project staff surveyed the villages and classified the households on the basis of immediate needs. Next, relief goods, e.g. seed, clothes, corrugated iron sheet and bamboo were provided : for free to the poor, against some payment to others. Those who had sided with the Pakistan army were excluded from benefits.

During the relief operation the Project established the

organizational and goodwill platform which it engaged in multifaceted community development in the region in 1973. Its models were the primary village cooperatives and the central *thana*-level cooperative which had been tried out for some time under the auspices of the Comilla Rural Development Academy.

At this stage, the Project had several pillars. One was the rule that, in principle, all villagers, rich and poor, could participate in all activities. This was reflected in the construction of *gonokendra* or people's centres. Another pillar was the functional education programme. This began with merely teaching literacy and numeracy, but in due course became more oriented towards the everyday problems of especially the poor participants. Eventually, functional education to a large extent implied raising awareness of the setting of such problems and translating this into possible lines of action. Next, there were an agricultural programme, a health and family planning programme (including a health insurance scheme) and credit facilities. In the meantime, an extensive and elaborate organizational structure was set up, including a number of camps from where Project workers covered the villages assigned to them. Such camps consisted of a few thatched or C.I. sheet buildings erected next to a village or *thana* headquarters.

The community development phase lasted till the second half of 1976. Then the Project was redirected towards a target-group approach. From then on, Project activities were meant for the poor and for them only. This implied the dismantling of the cooperative and the formation of new groups. Such groups consisted of men or women of more or less the same class. Eligible were those with no or hardly any land, who economically depended on selling their manual labour and who held no position of power in their village society.

Functional education was continued for some years to come, group savings were stimulated, and awareness raising through confrontations with the village elite gained a prominent place as a Project strategy. The agricultural programme was largely phased out, though some forms of collective support remained. The health programme was changed and is still there at a lower key. Supply of credit, though only on a collective basis and in addition to group savings, remained till 1981. From 1978 onwards, more and more Project personnel were withdrawn and camps were closed down.

At the same time a supra-village organization of landless people was built up. In late 1979 the various village groups started to have joint meetings. The following years these were institutionalized and in 1982 the decision was taken to have a formal, paid, Secretariat to run the supra-village organization. Presently, there is a system of policy-making central meetings of delegates who each represent a number of villages in the same Union. Such meetings are prepared by the Secretariat, with support from a permanent advisory council of experienced group members. The Secretariat also has an out-reach structure of paid area workers, among whom

Mrs. Hasina from Jaipur. The salaries of Secretariat members and area workers are secured from payments by the groups, but possible deficits are still guaranteed by the NGDO. In addition to their payment towards the administrative cost, the groups also contribute to a number of funds which are, respectively, meant for financing of development activities, emergency support of individual members, and as a kind of fall back provision for groups to draw on when they are involved in conflicts with the village power elite. Lately, the Secretariat has begun to investigate documentary evidence on access to *khas* land in the region, in order to formulate a coherent policy in this respect.

Though their external relations have changed, the groups still form the organizational backbone of the Project. Those groups which are still active presently get support from both the Secretariat and its area workers, and from the remaining Project worker who covers the village. But the Project coverage in a more narrow sense is becoming less and will eventually be taken over by supervision and support from the Secretariat. The organizational changes have made the groups more dependent to some extent, as control of some of the funds meant as support services for their members has been taken over by the Secretariat. Here we observe, in fact, an increase in the volume of possible support in exchange for a decrease in local decision-power.

To conclude this section on the Project we shall now briefly spell out the main elements of its inherent development approach since 1976. First, there has been considerable emphasis on the building of an organizational framework which would enable the poor to improve their living conditions by, especially, collective action. This was, second, supported by the training of leaders and other group members in skills required for a viable group-based organization. Moreover, by a process of functional education related to the everyday problems of the group members. Third, confrontations with the rural elite got much emphasis. They were both a means of getting access to land and to influential positions at the gateways of access to other assets, and a means to strengthen group cohesion. The basis for this policy was the conviction that people are primarily poor because of the specific socio-economic and political environment they live in. Changing this environment ought to be a primary aim of efforts to eradicate poverty in the countryside. Fourth, this process of change should be accomplished as much as possible by the poor themselves. The role of outsiders has to be an initiating, supportive and facilitating one. The Project staff chose to, if possible, never become directly involved in the village power struggles, in order not to obstruct the articulation of leadership among the poor. They also did not want to alienate the administration and, in that way, jeopardize the continuity of the Project. In this line also their reasonable and noncommittal behaviour towards the village elite should be understood. Fifth, savings and other economic activities should serve two purposes : enhance group cohesion and strengthen the economic backbone of the poor. Last, Project staff and their organization should withdraw from the region in the foreseeable future.

2. The Economic Position

In this section we shall investigate the effects of the emphasis on conscientization approach for the economic position of poor households that have participated in Project activities. The discussion will focus on several issues with indicator value, such as indebtedness, standard of living, and sources of income. First, however, we shall provide a few case studies, or economic profiles, of households which actively took part in Project activities, touching on indicators which will subsequently be elaborated on.

Case no.1 : *economic profile of a widow*

> Zarina (40) heads a family of four. One son is married and lives elsewhere in the village. Quite often he comes to her for financial support. She has been involved in Project activities for the last eight years. Economically her household rates A category. Her main source of income is petty trading. Throughout the year she moves around the village trying to sell dried fish, seasonal fruits, soap, oil, salt, etc. She also earns by giving out some land on *borga* to two male neighbours. She has received this land on a *rangjama* contract. She has a simple house made out of straw, mud and bamboo. She possesses two *sari*, one new, one torn, and two *piri* (tiny wooden stool).

She sleeps on a mat on the floor. She did not spend any money on the occasion of *Eid.* and says : "*Eid* is not for the poor". During the past years she could not afford to buy any land, cattle or ornaments. She has not seen any improvement in quality or quantity of her meals over the past years and describes her life as hardship. She is not indebted, but has no savings either. In time of need she will go to her women's group for support.

Case no.2 : *economic profile of an old wage labaurer.*

Amir Hussain, A category, about 60 years old, is a wage labourer who has to earn for himself, his wife, his sister, and his adopted granddaughter of age seven. Though he owns 0.70 acres of cultivable land, due to lack of animals and implements he cannot cultivate this himself and gives it out on *borga*. Usually he works for his well-to-do neighbour, a Union *Parishad* member. He told us to have come from a prosperous household in the old Mymensingh District but to have been robbed of his heritage by deceitful cousins. He owns a small house, which he was able to enlarge five years ago. He has got two *lungi* and his wife has two *sari*. The living quarter entails a cot and three *piri*. They also own a *dheki* for husking paddy. On the occasion of the most recent *Eid* he spent *taka* 150/-. A similar amount was spent on the primary school education of the grand daughter during one year. Last year he borrowed *taka* 500/- from relatives. No money was borrowed from members of the Project-groups which he and his wife joined eight years ago. When his wife was severely ill sometime ago, he went to the *mahajan* to borrow *taka* 300/-.

Vertical mobility

Investigating vertical social mobility is difficult, as van Schendel's sophisticated and interesting study (1981) shows. Though we do not possess the elaborate data needed to present a carefully balanced and properly founded statement on the issue, it is still possible to make some useful observations.

First, at the village level the proportion of the poorest category of households is considerably higher in Jaipur and Jaipur-West than in Nayagram, namely 84.6%, 83.9% and 61.7% (Table 2.1). When we take households from categories A and B together, the picture is more even, however. It does not seem too blunt a statement that, at least at an aggregate level, there are no indications of upward mobility in Jaipur if we look at the bottom of society.

This observation gets support from a comparison of main sources of income of sample households now and eight years ago (Table 2.3). If we rate wage labour lower than cultivation and trading and keep in mind that the category "others" here mainly stands for being dependent on a close relative or doing housework for others, we only can conclude that neither of the three samples shows clear signs of an overall upward mobility.

We also considered mobility from another angle, i.e., by asking the heads of our sample households to compare their present economic situation with that of eight years back (Table 2.4). The results at least support the view that on the whole participants in the Project have not been gaining economically, as compared to those who did not join. In sample S_1, most respondents perceived of their economic situation as being the same. In both the other samples the majority considered their situation as having improved.

Income

Wage labour, including both casual labour and working on an eight months' contract, is the principal source of income of poor heads of households in both villages. At village level we observed that wage labour is the main source of income of a larger proportion of the households in Jaipur than in Nayagram. This reflects our previous statement about Jaipur being the poorest of the two villages.

Cultivation, mainly on a *rangjama* contract, is the second main source of income mentioned by the poor ; petty trading is the third. This last activity is, however, about twice as prevalent among the poor men of Jaipur than among those in the control village.

The direct contribution of women to the total household income is most significant in Jaipur, especially among the women who joined the Project. Besides, among the income earning women, those engaged in petty trading (as compared to those working as a housemaid) were found mostly among the sample S_1 households.

Women may, of course, also contribute to the household income in other ways, such as kitchen gardening which, in addition to its impact on the menu, saves money. Further, poor women contribute considerably by collecting tubers from the *haor* and *bil* in November and December, and by gleaning after the harvest. Such activities are carried out especially by poor women from Jaipur. The Nayagram women are less mobile, as is described in the section on the position of women.

Standard of living

If we look at poverty in terms of access to land and ownership of tools and cattle to till the land, the following picture emerges. In Jaipur–West 79 out of 174 heads of households said they did not own any cultivable land, as compared to 25 out of 107 in Nayagram. This is another observation which reinforces our view of Jaipur's relative poverty. On the other side of the land distribution map, 24 heads of households in Jaipur-West told us to own more than 200 decimals of cultivable land, as to 38 in Nayagram. If we assume that the answers were equally reliable in both villages this points at more concentrated landownership in Jaipur-West.

As regards agricultural implements, we found that between 65% and 75% of the poor households in both villages did not own any plough or ladder. About the same number did not own any cow, bullock or, for that matter, goat. Poverty is, of course, also reflected in other matters, like housing, and availability of food. About 80% of the poorest (A category) households in both villages owned their living quarters. Such a house has a thatched roof, and walls of mud and bamboo. The more well-to-do have larger houses (though often smaller households) with sturdier walls and, often, a C.I. sheet roof. Some of the poor in Nayagram have been able to retain the C.I. sheets they were provided as relief goods in 1972. In Jaipur such items are virtually absent among the poor, as they had to sell them in the dire time of the *khas* land dispute. Except for size and overall quality the houses of the poor also stand out because of the need for repair. Three quarters of the households of A category in sample S_1 did not, for instance, make any improvement over the last eight years.

There are no indications that quality or quantity of meals have improved over the past years. In fact, we were often told the opposite, but this may be a consequence of idealizing the past, as it often was added that once milk and fish were abundant in the area. Presently, the meals of the poor follow a yearly cycle, during the lean period they only eat in the morning and the afternoon, in extreme cases even only once a day. At other times, there are three meals. The following cases nos. 3 and 4 are examples of the food schedule of two poor households, one Muslim, one Hindu, during one week of the better season of 1986. When studying it we should, of course, take into consideration what is said on men and women taking their food in the section on the position of women.

Case no. 3 : *food schedule of a poor Muslim household (A category, Sunamganj)*

Date	Breakfast	Lunch	Dinner
31.5.86	Rice, dry fish, *denga*, goat milk*	Rice prepared in the morning, dry fish, *denga* (veg.)	Rice, small fish curry
1.6.86	Rice, potato, small fish, goat milk	Rice prepared in the morning, small fish, potato	Rice, dry fish, *denga*
2.6.86	Cold rice, dry fish, goat milk	Cold rice prepared in the morning, jute leaf, goat milk	Rice, small fish
3.6.86	Rice, pulses, goat milk, banana	Cold rice prepared in the morning, pulses	Rice, small fish
4.6.86	Rice, jute leaf	Cold rice prepared in the morning, dry fish	Rice, small fish, *denga*
5.6.86	Rice, small fish, goat milk	Rice prepared in the morning, small fish	Rice, small fish, *denga*
6.6.86	Rice, dry fish, aram, goat milk	Rice prepared in the morning, dry fish	Rice, small fish, goat milk

*their ownership of a goat is rather exceptional

Case no. 4 : *food schedule of a poor Hindu household (A category, Sunamganj)*

Date	Breakfast	Lunch	Dinner
31.5.86	Cold rice, dry chilli	Rice, small fish, *denga*	Rice, fried potato
1.6.86	Puffed rice	Rice, pulses	Cold rice, dry fish
2.6.86	Rice, small fish	Cold rice, dry fish	Rice, potato
3.6.86	Rice, small fish	Flaked rice, puffed rice	Rice, pulses
4.6.86	Cold rice, banana	Rice, small fish	Cold rice, fried potato
5.6.86	Puffed rice, flaked rice, banana, milk	Rice, jute leaf	Rice, potato
6.6.86	Rice, small fish, *denga*, dry fish	Cold rice, small fish	Rice, pulses, fried potato

Little or no money is spent by the poor on *Eid* and other festive occasions. As Mrs. Zarina (Case no.1) said : "*Eid* is not for the poor". Those Hindus belonging to the Biswas community are an exception, however, as *puja* expenses are apportioned over all their households.

Some money is spent on dowry. During the last five years a total of 41 weddings took place among the A category households of all three samples together. In five cases dowry was given ; in eight cases it was taken. Usually, the dowry consists of goods, like rings, wooden furniture, bedding, watch, radio. Generally, it leads to indebtedness.

Indebtedness

The majority of all the sample households are regularly indebted. Each year, in the lean period, they are forced to borrow, usually from the *mahajan*. The traditional moneylender still holds a prominent position, even if additional sources of credit have been introduced. Not only do poor people go to them more often, they also take larger loans than from BRDB, bank, or private credit fund. Looking more specifically, we found that it is rather common to not always borrow from the same *mahajan*, but to have relations with a number of them. Besides, it was learned that people from Nayagram can select their *mahajan* more often in their own village than the poor of Jaipur do. This is related to relative scarcity of *mahajan* in Jaipur.

BRDB's role as provider of loans to the poor was found to be negligible in both villages during the lean period. None of the sample households in Jaipur and only two in Nayagram were found to have borrowed money from BRDB at that time.

Over the last five years the total of BRDB loans supplied to S_1, S_2 and S_3 sample households has been, respectively, six, four and nine. In fact, we observed that credit supplied by formal institutions like BRDB and Krishi

Bank is hard to get, small sized and relatively cheap. The *mahajan's* loan is, on the contrary, easy to get, expensive and, if needed, sizeable. His rate of interest varies, according to the season, between 25 and 100 percent a month, against the BRDB's 13% a year.

Among the households in our sample S_1, borrowing from relatives was found to be more common than from colleague group members. Still, the Project was often discussed in terms of credit provisions, namely when poor people reminisced about the time that credit was still supplied, be it on a collective basis, and stressed that this resource should be made available again.

Savings, assets and vulnerability

To the village poor savings means money in the bank, a handful of rice put aside and stored when preparing the daily meals, and money given out on loan. Additionlly, the female group members perceive of their participation in the Project's food security programme as savings. This entails taking paddy at harvest time and storing it jointly till the lean period. Each participant than receives what she has put in. Following their view of savings, the saving record of the poor is not impressive, though 22 out of 70 sample S_1 households participated in the Project's food security programme. Few households have outstanding loans and if they do, the amounts are small. Some Biswas families have saved a little money in the Krishi Bank.

In case of immediate disaster, which is rather different from the yearly returning seasonal disaster, savings are not an important back-up source which individual poor households can use. Both economic and domestic disasters hit hard and suddenly and usually it is the *mahajan* that people resort to for financial support. Another possibility is sale of cattle or other assets, but as we already mentioned, these are in very short supply among the poor. All three samples' poor households together mentioned eight cases over the last eight years when they sold assets to cover expenses due to death and illness : cattle, a house, C.I. sheets (twice) and ornaments (four times) were sold. Among the sample S_1 households only one case of support (*taka* 100/-) from the Project's emergency fund was reported for covering the costs of a domestic crisis. This happened some time before the funds control was transferred to the Secretariat. Additionally, the Project's funds were used, of course, to cover the costs of the *khas* land dispute, when this got to disaster-like proportions.

3. The Political Situation in the Villages

We shall investigate to what extent the development approach has resulted in a larger degree of political independence and bargaining power of households involved in the Project. This implies, first, a further elaboration on local-level politics. Next, we shall discuss the following issues ; interactions between the poor and the village elite ; possible changes in labour relation ; the voting behaviour of the poor in the elections of 1980, 1983, 1985 and 1986.

Factionalism and class conflict

Introduction of the Project drastically changed the nature

of village politics in Jaipur. The strongest man saw a female opponent emerge with a following consisting of both Muslims and Hindus. The strong personality of the female leader, in combination with her access to the Project staff and to the authorities gave her leadership elements of patronage and, to that extent made the group around her appear as a faction. However, the economic background of her followers and the nature of the issues fought about in the village arena make clear that we are dealing here primarily with a class conflict. The struggle about access to *khas* land, accordingly, can best be analyzed in such terms. Nevertheless, now and then factional elements intervene in the process of political conflict in the village. This happened, for instance, when part of the male group, mainly Mr. Anwar's relatives, realigned themselves with the opposite party. The election fights, which we shall discuss later, may be looked at slightly differently. They are, in fact, highly reminiscent of factional election disputes which are taking place regularly in villages all over South Asia. In the case of Jaipur, however, the disputes got a tougher edge, because they were episodes in a long term class conflict. Though structurally having similarities with factionalism, their meaning was a different one, going beyond a regular factionalist pattern.

In Nayagram we observed a more diffuse development. Here, factions only came about in 1983 and they hardly ever fought since then.

Case no. 5 : *the primary school donorship in Nayagram*

Many years ago Mr. Ram, a prominent villager,

took the initiative to establish a primary school, where for some time he also worked as a teacher. In 1984 the government decided that donorship made somebody eligible for a seat in the administration of a school and Mr. Ram claimed this seat. The leaders of the other faction did, however, strongly oppose his claim and pointed at contributions made to the school by others. When we left, the matter was still undecided. Mr. Ram remarked sadly : "once there was a time when I could guide the whole village. But now *matabar* are many and nobody abides by anybody". Referring to the leaders of the other faction he concluded : "a man can be a leader but to become a gentleman two to three generations are required."

The traditional *chan* (subcaste council covering several villages) is still functioning, in Nayagram e.g. in case of marriage arrangements and, the next case shows, occasionally as a mediator. Though the Project never mobilized the poor of Nayagram, traces of resistance against poverty conditions can be found there as well.

Case no. 6 : *the labour contract dispute in Nayagram*

One of Mr. Dulal's sons went on an eight months' contract service to the households of Mr. Manik. He was to receive 24 *maund* of paddy at the end of the contract, and an additional seven pieces of clothes. Board and lodging was also included in the contract. When his son started his duties, the father took four *maund* of paddy as an advance. A fortnight before the contract was over Dulal's son returned home in ill health. The employer arbitrarily deducted ten *maund* from the total wages due to non-fulfilment of contract obligations. In the ensuing quarrel Dulal and his son, belonging to A category, were strongly supported by members from A and B category households, belonging to both village factions. Eventually the matter was settled through mediation by the *chan*, on the initiative of a villager who belonged to a local leftist party and who strongly emphasized the class issue during the quarrel. The settlement, a penalty of one *maund* paddy for breaking the contract, was perceived by all involved as a gain for Dulal and his supporters.

Still, compared to the actions of poor people in neighbouring villages the resistance record of the poor of Nayagram is not impressive. They have, for instance, not been involved in any *khas* land dispute.

Case no. 7 : *khas land in Nayagram*

Since long, the well-to-do of Nayagram were using a piece of *khas* land for grazing purposes. This particular piece of land is situated near to a neighbouring village. In this village the Project had organized a group which in 1985 successfully occupied the Nayagram piece of *khas* land. They had tried to do so before, but then to no avail, as they met with fierce resistance. This time the Nayagram people were too divided to prevent occupation of the land, so the faction leaders told us. At no time did the poor of Nayagram take part in any efforts to get hold of their village *khas* land.

Everyday interaction between the poor and other villagers

In both villages, though most clearly so in Jaipur, the poor are behaving differently towards the elite than they used to do. When listening to more well-to-do villagers we often heard that the poor have become more articulate with regard to both the identification of their problems and the presentation of their argument. Like Mr. Raihan, a Jaipur *matabar* said : "they now have become aware of their rights and they never fail to present and enforce their legal rights. These days, the poor have begun to visit the village *salish* increasingly." What struck us most in this respect was the outspokenness of the poor about their experience that the village elite hardly ever do justice to them, as is, they say, shown by the embezzlement of public funds, among other things.

Such conflict cases as we already presented include clear indications, of course, of behaviour which is the opposite of acting docile or as "yes men." In case no. 6 it is, for instance, significant that Dulal did not seek mediation immediately when quarreling with a landowner, and that he openly alleged that his son fell ill because he had to work under too unfavourable conditions. Another case from Jaipur shows how these articulation of the poor had progressed considerably even before the *khas* land dispute started.

Case no. 8 : *the sacrifice of a cow*

As elsewhere, the rich Muslims of Jaipur traditionally used to sacrifice a cow at the occasion of *Eid-Ul-Azha* and distribute one third of the meat to the village poor. After the poor became organized and more outspoken about their rights the yearly distribution of free meat was stopped. Then, the village poor arranged to sacrifice their own cow, but the village elite objected to this, claiming that insolvent people have no right to do a thing like this. Mrs. Hasina put the matter before some *Maulvi* (learned religious men) who decided in favour of the poor. The poor from then on have been performing a cow sacrifice every year.

Labour relations in the villages

On the whole, in both villages labour conditions have not improved during recent years. Though there have been increases in money payments for casual labour, these barely, if at all, kept up with inflation. No changes in conditions of the locally prevailing eight months' contract were reported. Though it is difficult to make a solid statement on the basis of our material, there is a strong impression that, especially, the ample availability of labourers is a decisive factor regarding prevailing conditions of labour and access to land. Moreover, relative scarcity of land in combination with unpredictable but high incidence of adverse climatic conditions has made *rangjama* contracts rather popular among landowners. A common pattern of managing the tilling of one's land seems to be : to give out some on *rangjama* against a fixed prepaid amount of cash, to take on a labourer for odd jobs on an eight months' contract, and to hire migrant labourers for peak activities.

For the poor households it all means that the economic basis of their livelihood has not improved lately. That is, unless they began to earn an additional income via women's work or through one of their members participating in a private credit scheme. In fact, most of the poor are still largely dependent on agriculture and on the landowners who set the rules. During four months of the year there is, except fishing for household consumption, no agricultural income earning possible for most of them.

The elections

During the last four elections (for background see Blair, 1985) the voting behaviour of the poor in Jaipur and in Nayagram has been quite different. In Jaipur the election campaigns were, next to the *khas* land dispute, main issue in the ongoing class conflict. In fact, the mobilization of the group members around the various elections signified a major Project mobilization strategy.

At the 1980 *Gram Sarkar* (village government) elections the members of both the male and female group rallied behind their own candidate, Mrs. Hasina. When during the voting it became apparent that there was a good chance of her being elected, the opposition started a turmoil. Next, the polling officer stopped the polling and left the village. After some time, he announced the election results from the then *thana* headquarters : Mrs. Hasina's opponent had been elected. Members of the groups complained about the outcome at high administrative levels, but without any positive result. Eventually the *Gram Sarkar* scheme evaporated without ever having been operational.

In 1983, the Secretariat decided to contest the Union *Parishad* elections : Mrs. Hasina was again nominated a candidate. In Jaipur's Union the election ended in fight and chaos, with the administration again interfering in an election which might well have come out in favour of Mrs. Hasina.

In 1985 and 1986 the elections concerned high level administrative bodies, i.e. the *Upazila* Council and the National Assembly. The Village poor belonging to the Project groups rallied in both cases behind the opponent of the candidate supported by Mr. Anwar, their archenemy. In Nayagram, the situation was rather different. In 1980 all villagers voted unitedly. In 1983 a factional split occurred ; in 1985 and 1986 all villagers again were able to support a common candidate. At no time did the village poor have a separate voting strategy.

4. The Position of the Women

In the following pages we shall investigate (changes in) the power balance between husbands and wives with regard to, especially, economic decision-making in the household. We shall also discuss how women are treated in general and which degrees of freedom they have to move around. First, we present some cases of poor women's conditions, next we move to the discussion.

Case no.9 : *three poor widows*

I

Samata (A category, sample S_1) presently lives together with her unmarried daughter (aged 16) and, since half a year, also with her married daughter, and her husband and child. Both she and her son-in-law are engaged in petty-trading. She sells dried fish, salt, matches, fruit, soap and other household items. Previously, when her husband was still alive, his wage labour was the major source of income. Samata is really poor. She owns one *sari* only and nothing was spent on the occasion of *Eid*. No dowry was given on her daughter's wedding. She took a *taka* 100/- loan from a *mahajan* for her business, but gave some paddy on loan as well. Usually, she takes the economic decisions, though she sometimes consults her unmarried daughter, who also helps her in keeping the accounts. She also consults her other daughter and son-in-law, if they are available. She is quite positive about their future prospects : by hard work they will pull through. She wants both of her daughters to have two sons plus two daughters, all of whom should be educated.

II

Kitabjan (A category, sample S_2) heads a five member household. She earns from petty trade and by working as a housemaid. Her son is a wage labourer. She is not indebted, but was able to provide a loan of 10 *maund* of paddy to a neighbour. She owns two *sari* and spent *taka* 25/- at the last *Eid*.

She discusses all economic decisions with her adult son. In all the elections she voted according to her own preference. Hard work and austerity are her suggestions for the removal of poverty. She is rather positive about the future and wants the next generation to have education and try for a government job. She believes the poor can and should help each other to change their conditions.

III

Komola (A category, sample S_3) works as a housemaid. Three of her sons work as wage labourers, as did her late husband. She discusses all economic decisions with her sons, as was the case when they recently take a *taka* 1000/- loan from a *mahajan*. But they consult her as well before taking a loan. She believes their future holds promises and points out that government could play an important role by distributing the *khas* land to the poor.

Economic decision-making

Women are earning an outside income in both villages ; their proportion is only slightly higher in Jaipur-West (see Table 2.5). Additionally, we found that Jaipur working women from Project related households were clearly more involved in earning money than women from samples S_2 and S_3, who more often worked as housemaid and accordingly were paid in kind. When asking the earning women how decisions on spending their income were taken, women from Jaipur seemed to be more influential than those of Nayagram. Due to the small numbers of respondents involved we have to be careful here, however.

Women from sample S_1 were considerably more involved in taking outside loans, mostly from BRDB. Many of them said to decide on the timing, amount and use of such loans themselves. The sample S_1 women also more often indicated that they were surely having a say when their husbands were going to borrow.

Marriage of children

We were told that even a few years back the opinion of women did not count much in decisions regarding marriages, but that things were changing now. However, the actual information we got on the matter does not seem to support this strongly. Daughters who marry are yet not asked to give their opinion on their husband to be. Men clearly play a larger role in matchmaking than the women, both among the Muslims and the Hindus. If women have a say in the choice of a partner for their children, their influence is clearly largest when a daughter is to be married.

General treatment of women

Regarding meals all Hindu women told us that they took theirs after the men, who also got most and best quality food. Most of the Muslim women in the Jaipur samples follow the same pattern, except for a few from sample S_1, who said to have eaten together or before the men ; still, they as well gave their men most and best of the meal. The proportion of these women is too small for us to be able to state that a new trend is emerging.

The investigation of incidence and fear of divorce was not very illuminating, as it only applied to Muslim households. In samples S_1 and S_2 together two women and two men had previously been divorced. Most Muslim women we interviewed said they were not afraid of divorce.

Quarrels between men and women occur regularly in most households and we have a strong impression that their incidence is highest among the poorest. However, we did not come across any case of a man beating his wife. Some members of the female group in Jaipur indicated that incidence of beating had been considerably higher before the introduction of the Project.

Freedom to move around

In both villages women are moving around outside their own compound, *para* and even village, though there are differences in the nature and scope of this freedom. First, as compared to Jaipur women, the Nayagram women were far more often reported to have to ask permission to leave *para* or village. Among poor women of Jaipur such questions are hardly posed at all. Second, poor Jaipur women do leave their village far more often than those in Nayagram, mainly for economic purposes, or for meetings and demonstrations. Among poor women from Jaipur, the mobility is most significant among the Muslim women.

Women of both villages leave their house, *para* or village to visit relatives, shrines, *puja* gatherings, fetch water, take a bath, go shopping or go to their outside working site. In addition, poor Muslim women in Jaipur go out to collect firewood or tubers, gleaning, hawking. They attend meetings or, occasionally, a training or conference. Poor Jaipur women's larger mobility which was certainly not restricted to participants in the Project is strongly related to their relatively larger share of outdoor economic activities, which also means that they have to shoulder a heavier work burden. The Jaipur women who have joined the Project at times are showing quite radical behaviour. So, they played a prominent role at election time and were heavily involved in the *khas* land case. It was they, for instance, who began the transplanting of rice, traditionally a man's job, when the *khas* land had been occupied. This strategy had been chosen because it was rightly believed that the village elite would hesitate to fight off the women. The following case is another example of the change in women's behaviour.

Case no. 10. *the gherao of the doctor*

In 1985 the chief medical officer of the local government health center, located just over a kilometer from each of the study villages, refused to treat a male patient from a nearby village without him paying a fee in advance. This demand was, of course, against government rules. Women, and some men, from Project groups in four villages took action on the initiative of Mrs. Hasina from Jaipur. They went to the doctor's place and surrounded it, till in the end he promised to treat the patient free and not to repeat his bad behaviour.

5. Organization and Unity of the Poor

Jaipur was included in the Project from the beginning. Female and male cooperatives were set up in, respectively, 1974 and 1975, and later converted into socio-economically more homogeneous groups. In the early 1980s the male group was at the peak of its strength with more than 100 members. This was the period of the struggle for access to *khas* land. The number of members had increased decisively as a consequence of entrance of men from the Biswas community. They had been allotted certain legal rights to the *khas* land, but until then had failed to exercise them. A deal was made with the male group : the Biswas men would join them and for some time share with them all benefits when the access would be secured. During the conflict, which lasted several years, the group was an organizationally and morally strong collective, becoming stronger in the process. This was especially so in 1981/82 when for one season access was gained and the land could be cultivated. But de facto access was then lost again. The overall financial costs of the conflict were extremely high, particularly because of the 20 (false) courtcases that the opponents got registered against group members. The group's emergency fund was exhausted and individual members lost savings and had to sell some assets. Eventually the costs and the gains did prove not to be in balance and members became demoralized and disinterested.

In fact, though there have been some minor economic group activities in later years, i.e., landlevelling and road plantation work, the fight for the *khas* land has been one of two main preoccupations of the male group. The other, intermittent, activities were the election campaigns of 1980, 1983, 1985 and 1986, when both the male and the female group rallied behind a common candidate. At the time of our census (and of the 1986 elections) the male group actually had become defunct, but the female group was still rather active. To a considerable extent this must be contributed to the leadership of Mrs. Hasina, a Muslim lady with only primary education, who has become well known in the whole Project region. In the beginning of 1986 the female group counted 70 members, just over 30 of whom had formed a BRDB saving and credit cooperative. The female group is, further, involved in health education and in putting together a food security fund. The group meets rather frequently, though less often than the seven days' routine of the past. Though occasionally backbiting occurs within the group, splits do not really mature. The group's chance of survival seems rather high as long as Mrs, Hasina's leadership remains secure, so that activities are stimulated.

Other economic groups

In both villages, BRDB is providing loans to registered societies. In Jaipur, there is the aforementioned women's society, which provides individual poor women with credit, while using the organizational backbone of the Project group. Nayagram has a female BRDB society as well, but this one is dominated by well-off women; the few poor members have been selected to do the necessary administrative work. The society, established in 1982 is currently dormant and has been so since 1984.

Case no. 11 : *the breaking up of female BRDB society*

> The uneducated manager of the society went to the BRDB office to return an amount of *taka* 5900/-. Later she realized that she had not got any receipt. She went back to see the cashier, but he excused himself. She continued to press him to provide the receipt during subsequent visits, but he never did. One day she found that he had been transferred. The issue led to gossiping and ultimately a near breakup of the society. Moreover, the BRDB has been hesitant to provide any new loans.

There are two male BRDB societies in Nayagram and one in Jaipur. Though these societies have a sprinkling of poor members, they mainly are a vehicle for more well-to-do villagers to get loans.

In both villages a male private credit fund has sprung up. About three years ago eight Nayagram men independently formed a credit cooperative. Six of them rate A category, one B and one D. The D category man contributes two shares, so they call it a nine member committee. Essentially, they run a moneylending business, extending loans against interest to both members and others, but without taking collateral. The comparable Jaipur committee comprises of 12 young men, all of A category. In 1986 both societies suffered from the the consequences of the bad weather, which made it hard to realize repayment of their loans.

Views of participating in the Project

As we have seen, the Project has rather drastically changed its character over the years. These changes have left different resentment scars among the Jaipur villagers. In the beginning those Muslims who supported the Pakistan army were excluded from the provision of relief goods. Some of them still perceive of this as an injustice. Many of those excluded, together with others, joined the cooperatives set up in the next phase. In this period the better-off benefitted most, but they had to leave when in 1976 the Project changed direction again. In Nayagram Project activities were stopped after the relief phase, but we did not encounter any hard feelings there about their being shut out. In 1981 the Project discontinued provision of credit, which is still felt by many as a wrong decision.

Then there are, of course, the poor who changed sides during the *khas* land dispute and those who suffered tremendous losses at the time and saw their male group disintegrate. The one time leader of this group still clearly bore a grudge against the Project, which according to him in fact made them fall out of the frying pan into the fire. His sister, active in the women's group, saw things quite differently. She pointed out that those poor who are critical of the Project are not yet fully aware of its important contribution. They do not yet understand that it is because of the Project that they can presently open their mouth, contest elections, sit in the *salish* and receive proper treatment from administrative and village *matabar*.

Though the Project's female group as such shows an outstanding unity, it is not without strains. We heard complaints against its leaders, who would not properly maintain funds, distribute benefits or inform about coming activities. Some members from the village's eastern side complained that those from the other side, where Mrs. Hasina lives, get more benefits. But nobody was found to raise such criticism in front of the leaders. When one day a member was giving us such a negative comment, she abruptly stopped when one of the group's leaders joined. These leaders are quite laconic about the complaints. Their reproach is that members often have too high expectations. Further, they point out that those who criticize are mainly peripheral members, "some of whom do not even know that they have actually dropped out."

We also inquired about women's motives to join Project

groups. The answers ranged from achieving self-sufficiency to getting mental peace, and checking population growth. But the objective which was clearly stated most often, was the possibility to get a loan. Next in line came the objective of improving one's financial position through saving and in this way ensuring a better future. In third place came the motive of learning how to live together better, followed by, fourth, to get help in distress and, fifth, to get to know the why of exploitation, including how to stop it.

Collective action

A major Project strategy has been collective action as a means to both increasing unity among the poor and reaching the goal of improving their position. In the previous pages we already discussed some collective actions, like the *khas* land dispute and the election campaigns. We shall now, briefly, mention some additional points about joint economic activities and confrontations.

(*a*) *Joint economic activities*

In the past, both Project groups collectively took up some economic activities, like landlevelling and planting trees along the road (the men) ; knitting of nets and paddy husking (the women). None of these ventures has really been a great success ; usually the story about them shows a path with pitfalls. The women's group, for instance, took a loan of *taka* 27000/- from the Project in 1980, which it used to purchase paddy at the time when its price was low. They stored it to sell again during the lean period, but that year an odd thing happened ; the price went down. They then decided not to sell the paddy but to distribute it amongst the group members at a price of *taka* 130/- per *maund.* In the process some members failed to pay the price. Still, the group made a profit of *taka* 4000/-which was then again converted into paddy, which was used to start the group's food security fund.

Of course, the two private credit funds we mentioned are also forms of collective economic action, as are the activities of men who groupwise engage in earthcutting, fishing, sowing, weeding, harvesting, stacking of straw and building of houses.

At one point, collective economic action gets a strong aspect of mutuality, as when neighbours assist in house repair, or when women help each other out with house cleaning at the occasion of a wedding or a *puja.* As to mutuality among the poor it has, further, to be realized that they have minimal possibilities to support others financially. It is, therefore, hardly surprising that only few households in our three samples mentioned having extended a loan to others recently or that Project group members hardly feature as a source of financial support in time of need.

(b) confrontations

The *khas* land was the longest and most dramatic confrontation in Jaipur. For many of the poor it also was a most traumatic experience, as it brought about unity, as well as disunity and, in the end, a lot of misery. Still, its significance has been considerable for at least three reasons. First, because of the alignment of the Hindu and Muslim poor in the village. Second, because of its demonstration value. The case became widely known in the region and the leaders of both parties got symbolic proportions, one representing good, the other evil. Third, the Jaipur men involved were supported by the women and also, both financially and morally, by groups from other villages. Similarly, on other occasions, both the Jaipur groups rendered support when the poor of other villages got involved in a class conflict.

Still, there have been quite some more occasions on which the poor and the elite of Jaipur confronted each other. We already mentioned the action against the government doctor, and the action to get the opportunity to sacrifice a cow at *Eid.* We shall conclude this section with yet another case.

Case no. 12 : *mismanagement of a government grant*

> In 1980, a local *matabar* used government wheat meant to be paid as Food for Work in a local employment scheme, to pay labourers for the improvement of his house. Mrs. Hasina took up this case and mobilized the female group to put this matter right, She also got support from members of the male group. She went to the Union *Parishad* member under whose jurisdiction the wheat was issued and pointed out that something very wrong was happening. Members of both groups accompanied her on her visits to the authority. Ultimately, the big man

involved admitted that he must have made a mistake and the wheat was then used for its proper purpose.

6. The Worldview of the Poor

Roots of Poverty

At one point during the often lengthy interviews we asked the heads of households and their wives, or the women heading a household, to reflect on their present conditions and their future. We inquired what they considered to be the main causes of poverty in general, and of their personal poverty. We did not put a limit to the number of causes they were allowed to mention, nor did we attach any value to the sequence of causes referred to. As many causes were put forward we had to group them in clusters, in order to sight their regularities. We distinguished six clusters of answers. The first covers both day-to-day burdens, like a disabled wife, and sudden mishaps and burdens, such as disease and crop failure, but also marriage expenses. The next cluster regards the will of God, fate, *karma* as causes of poverty. Then there are two clusters of economic causes. The first, plain economic causes, covers answers which state a plain insufficiency or economic problem, such as scacrity of land or agricultural imputs. The second, political-economic causes covers all answers which referred to the distribution of (access to) resources in terms of injustice and exploitation. Though there were a few borderline cases, in general the assignment of an answer to one of the two clusters was no problem.

The fifth cluster contains self-accusatory answers, such as "lack of determination" and "lack of wisdom." Finally, there is a cluster "no opinion."

Before we look into the findings of each of the study areas separately, we want to draw attention to an observation which applies to both the areas. Many respondents in all samples mentioned several causes of poverty in their answer, which to outsiders may seem to be rather contradictory. So, they might combine "fate" with causes like "unequal distribution of land" or "exploitation." This is, of course, less of a contradiction than it appears to be. It merely reflects the nature of their own existence, where they are, for instance, trapped between manmade and natural disasters. There is, evidently, much more to say about this matter, but this is not the proper place to do so.

When we look at the tables regarding the Sunamganj villages, it strikes us, first of all, that about one third of both male and female respondents in sample S_1 professed not to have an opinion on the roots of general poverty. An explanation for this unexpected phenomenon is not easily available. Two suggestions may be made : one regards the higher level of education in Nayagram, but how to explain then the low "no opinion" response among sample S_2 : the other is that in awareness-raising education the Project has taken individual poverty as a point of departure, which has helped this to become the major perspective to look at poverty among the participating poor.

Next, we see that, in general, samples S_1 and S_2 put

more emphasis on political-economic causes, whereas in sample S_3 plain economic causes were most often mentioned. It is, further remarkable that political-economic causes got a relatively high score also in Nayagram.

If we differentiate between men and women there is especially a difference shown in the pattern of sample S_1 : women put more emphasis on plain economic factors.

Finally, a finding which is different from what might be expected is the relatively low number of answers referring to fate, *karma* or the will of God ; their prevalence is even lowest in sample S_3. Possibly, in the interpretations of our respondents plain economic factors and disaster belong to this realm as well.

The distribution of answers on causes of personal poverty is different from that just presented. Here, disasters and plain economic causes, both unalterable by the poor, score highest in all three samples. Two other remarkable general findings must be noticed. One is high prevalence of self-accusatory answers in sample S_3. Another is that sample S_1 and to a lesser extent also S_2, show higher prevalence of political-economic causes than self-accusatory one's, which is the opposite of what the S_3 distribution shows. Still, this difference is not large.

If we compare men and women, the most striking observation is that in sample S_1 far more women than men mentioned plain and political-economic causes, which seems to point at them being a bit more articulate.

Solutions to poverty

When asked how they would formulate solutions to the problem of poverty our respondents again gave a variety of answers. After clustering, however, this variety, though as such an interesting feature, subsided into a readable pattern. Before discussing this, we want to elucidate two of the clusters mentioned in tables 2.10 and 2.11. One is "self-change" ; this covers answers like "limiting the size of one's family" and "working harder." The other is "despair", which refers to people expressing their view of no change at all being possible or having no time to think about the future. It may appear an important result that, with regard to both general and personal poverty, only few respondents reacted in a despairing way. In fact, it is shown by these and other findings that most people appear to have at least some confidence in the future. Still, we have to be a bit careful here, as answers pointing at God's will or fate, or stressing plain economic solutions, will to the extent that they are the expression of powerlessness, often border on despair.

Regarding general poverty, a few respondents in samples S_1 and S_3 had opinion on possible solutions, with highest prevalence among women from sample S_3. Next, we see that responses from samples S_1 and S_3 show a rather similar pattern, with government action, self-change and political-economic changes ranking highest. Among the women only, the picture differs to the extent that sample S_1 women mentioned political-economic changes most often of all the factors, while these had a very low prevalence among answers of women from samples S_2 and S_3. Among the men, sample S_2 stands out its high preference for self-change.

A puzzling outcome is the low prevalence in especially sample S_3 of answers referring to fate or God's will as a way to end poverty, while in sample S_2 such answers score quite high. In other words, both in this respect, and in the difference in emphasis on political-economic factors, the two control samples show a considerable difference. It might be a suggestion to look for an explanation here in differences in religious background

With regard to personal poverty, sample S_2 takes the place of S_3 with regard to "no opinion", with the score of sample S_1 remining about the same. Here, again, we observe much similarity between the total samples S_2 and S_3 with respect to the three clusters getting most emphasis. Again, sample S_2 rather stands out, this time with high scores for "plain economic changes" and "God's will and fate." In all three samples "self-change" was mentioned most often as the way to end poverty. Political-economic changes got high ranking in answers from sample S_1 women (to be expected) and sample S_3 men (rather surprising). Here as well, samples S_2 and S_3 are each other opposite at some points.

Views of the future

We also asked our respondents to reflect on their future situation and that of their children. It was striking that most of them, men and women of all samples equally, expected their sons and grandsons to own land, or more land than the household did at present. When asked how this should be accomplished a preference for hard work was shown in the answers, with "by government help" and "through education" in second place. Cooperative activities were only mentioned once as a means to acquire more land.

Another issue we asked the respondents to comment on was the way in which they would like their children to earn an income. Like in the case of the previous questions, we did not put a limit to their answers. At the bottom of the list were the professions, like lawyer, doctor, and, also, teacher. The answers which scored highest were, actually, of two kinds. One indicating the way to gaining a good position, the other the position itself. Education was mentioned often in all samples as the vehicle to a brighter future. Except in sample S_1, its prevalence was, incidentally, highest among the men. As to the position aspired, many respondents would like to see their children in a government's job, though mostly so in sample S_1. An office job ("service") was another favourite, best liked by samples S_2 and S_3. Business, in third place, was liked slightly more by sample S_1 men, with all the women scoring the same. Finally, cultivation, low in the lists, was primarily mentioned by women, and most so by sample S_2 and S_3 women.

II

As we have seen, many poor have high expectations about improvement of their situation. Things may change, they think, and probably will for their children. They do not despair but, on the contrary, have indentified a number of venues along which their conditions could be improved.

A final observation we want to make pertains to their confidence and expectations with regard to outside help. When we inquired about this the majority pointed out that government had done nothing for them, but *should* provide work, credit, *khas* land or support in general. Most of them even had a dimmer look of the political parties : they neither have done nor can do anything for them was the general view. They also did not come forward with normative statements on actions of the political parties.

In fact, such observations indicate that the poor feel very much on their own. Except for a small number of respondents in the sample S_1, the picture remains the same when we include their views on the support from the side of the NGDO which was active in the area.

A final remark must be added here. When asking about future help from government, political parties and the NGDO, especially many women vented no opinion, though least so in sample S_1. As to the role of political parties and NGDO a considerable number of men joined the women in saying not a word. We feel this finding is important too, as it shows how little outside agencies figure in the poor's analysis of their situation.

Positive and isolated are, accordingly, two catch words to describe some of the worldview of the poor. They expressed hope for and expectations of change for the better. They see ways to reach a better future, but at the same time are well aware that most of these are not realistic. Moreover, and this is a third element of their worldview we want to stress, they did not express much confidence in their own collective efforts as a way to bring about desired changes. But there was an exception to this, namely the women belonging to the Jaipur Project group. At different occasions they radiated a superior self-confidence and showed to view their group as a corner stone to the realization of their aspirations.

MAP NO. 4

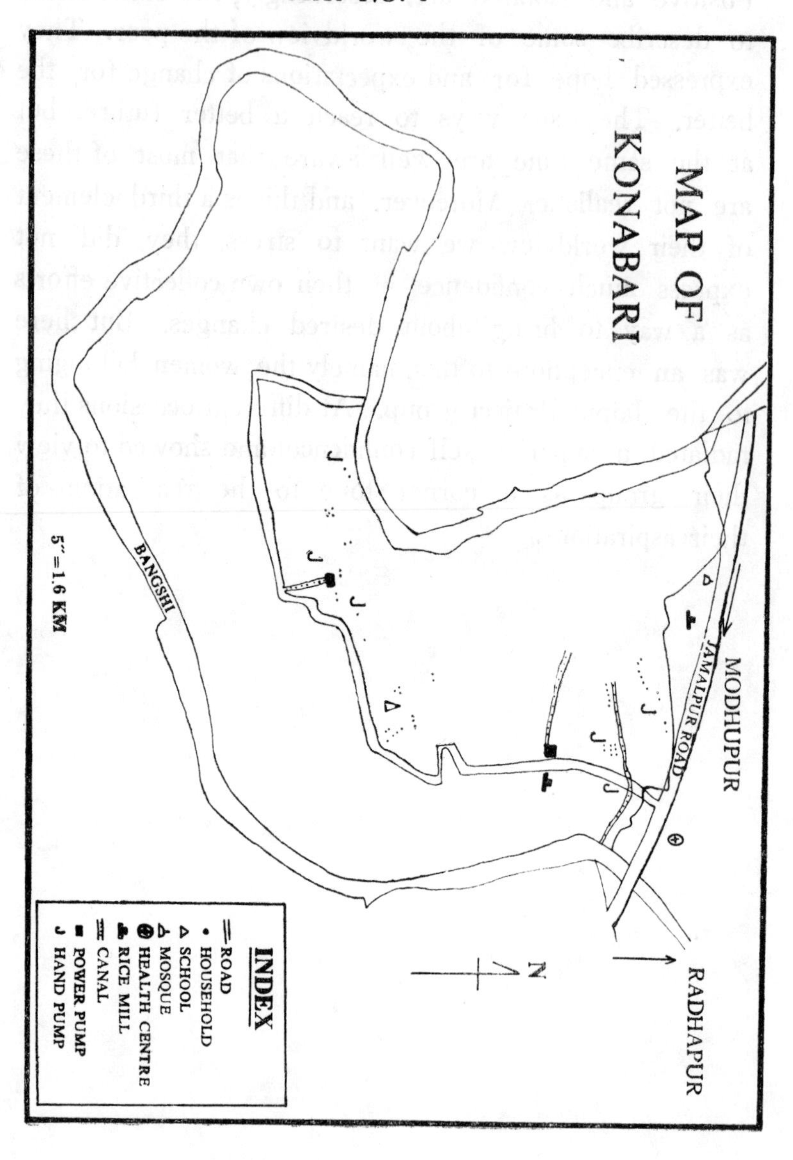
MAP OF
KONABARI
MODHUPUR
JAMALPUR ROAD
RADHAPUR
N
BANGSHI
5" = 1.6 KM
INDEX
ROAD
HOUSEHOLD
SCHOOL
MOSQUE
HEALTH CENTRE
RICE MILL
CANAL
POWER PUMP
HAND PUMP

MAP NO .5

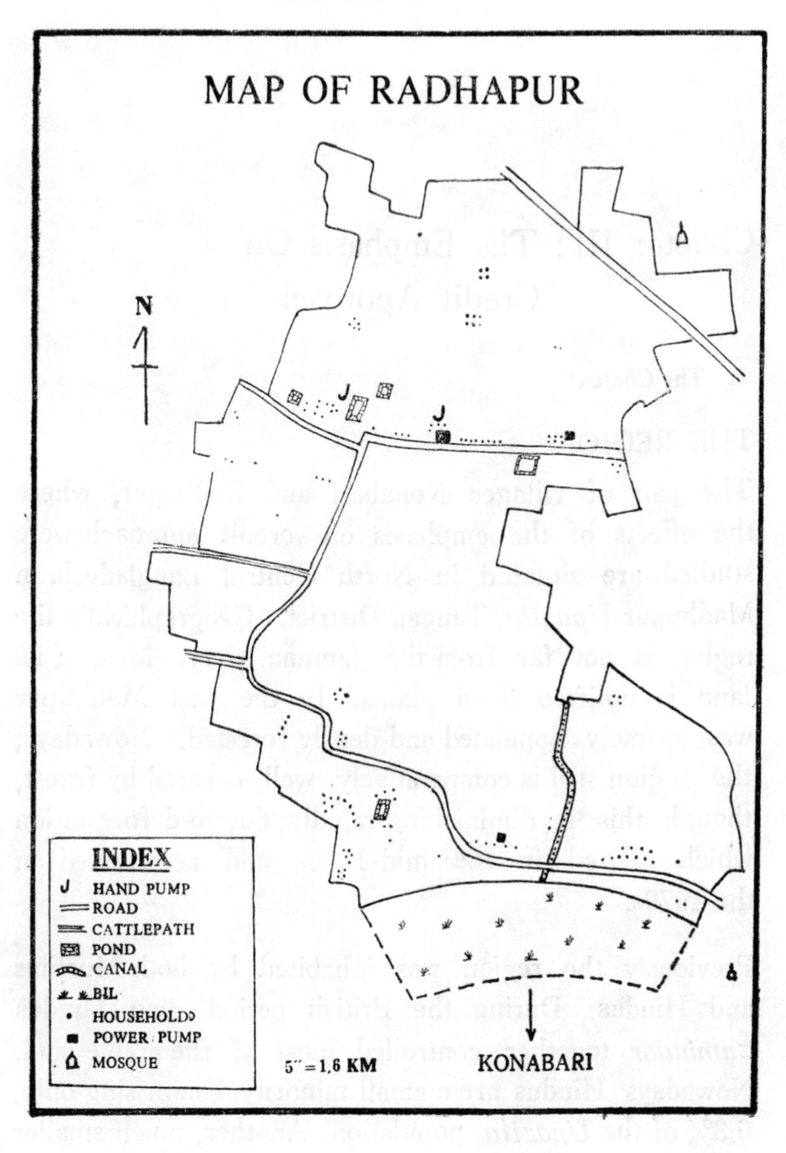
MAP OF RADHAPUR
N
J
J
INDEX
HAND PUMP
ROAD
CATTLEPATH
POND
CANAL
BIL
HOUSEHOLD
POWER PUMP
MOSQUE
5" = 1,6 KM
KONABARI

Chapter III : The Emphasis On Credit Approach

1. The Context

THE REGION

The pair of villages Konabari and Radhapur, where the effects of the emphasis on credit approach were studied are situated in North Central Bangladesh, in Madhupur *Upazila*, Tangail District. Geographically the region is not far from the Jamuna river. Most of its land is uplifted flood plains. In the past Madhupur was sparsely populated and densly forested. Nowadays, the region still is comparatively well covered by forest, though this is diminishing rapidly, due to deforestation which started in the mid-1960s and accelerated in the 1970s.

Previously the region was inhabited by both Muslims and Hindus. During the British period two Hindus *zamindar* together controlled most of the arable land. Nowadays Hindus are a small minority, comprising only, 6.3% of the *Upazila* population. Another, much smaller minority numbering less than one per cent are the tribals, mainly Garos.

Before the 1960s one, or at the most two crops of rice and a jute crop were grown on most of the cultivated land. Then, from the mid 1960s power pump irrigation and the Green Revolution in rice cultivation were introduced, leading to multiple cropping and crop diversification. Presently three rice crops, jute (to a diminishing extent) and wheat (since the mid 1970s) are grown, next to minor cash crops like jackfruit, pineapple, mustard, pulses, turmeric, ginger and potatoes. Fishing and dairy are only done for subsistence. The agricultural year 1984-85 was, except for wheat, a relatively good year in the area.

Madhupur is the only urban centre worth mentioning in the *Upazila.* Its distance from Tangail is 48 kms and from Dhaka 144 kms. The town is mainly a trading centre, which was boosted by the agricultural changes which were just mentioned and recently also gained administrative importance. There are some small industries, such as brick kilns, rice mills and handlooms. Further, there are two cinemas, while three others are under construction.

THE VILLAGES

The Project Village

General

Konabari is situated on the bank of the river Bangshi, one km. from Madhupur and six kms. from the control village. Both villages can be reached by minor road throughout the year. Originally Konabari was mainly a Hindu village, but now only three Hindu households are left. At the time of Partition (1947) the entire Hindu population departed for Cooch Bihar, now part of India. They changed places with the Muslims of a village there and 70% of Konabari's present Muslim population originate from this Cooch Bihar village. Konabari's layout and surroundings can be seen in map 4.

Population

Konabari is a small village, with 72 households encompassing 391 people. Among them, 206 men and 185 women were counted, which corresponds with a male/female ratio of 111. Under fifteens constitute 39.4% of the population. Among the heads of households 76.4% did not receive formal education ; among the adult women the corresponding percentage is 78.4. The economic categorization of the population, which includes a strikingly low percentage of A category households, can be seen in Table 3.1.

Agriculture

Until the middle of the 1960s only an *aus* rice crop was grown in Konabari. Then, after introduction of power pumps and high yielding varieties an *amon* and a *boro* crop were added. Now most cultivators grow two or three rice crops, while an increasing number grows wheat as well. Some jute is cultivated too. As to the *robi* crops, there are mustard, raddish, pulses and vegetables, like before. An innovation is the introduction of bananas, which are grown commercially on a small scale.

The agricultural transformation with regard to the major

Table 3.1 : Economic categorization of households and people in Konabari and Radhapur

	Konabari				Radhapur			
	No	%	No	%	No	%	No	%
A	20	27.8	87	22.3	47	38.2	163	27.4
B	35	48.6	165	42.2	40	32.5	188	31.7
C	12	16.7	85	21.7	27	22.0	158	26.6
D	5	6.9	54	13.8	9	7.3	85	14.3
Total	72	100.0	391	100.0	123	100.8	594	100.0

Source : Census November—December 1985

food crops had an important impact on labour requirements. There are more crops, and more and shorter growing cycles. As a result there are multiple transplanting, weeding and harvesting operations throughout the year. This implies a larger labour demand, as well as a different demand schedule. Besides, the timing of the lean periods has changed. There are two of these now, one before the *amon* harvest and one before the *boro* harvest.

Initially the cultivators in Konabari irrigated their land with water which they lifted by power pump from the river Bangshi. In the mid 1970s this practice was abandoned, however, as the water level fell due to the operation of the Farakka barrage in India. From then on the power pumps–there are three of them in the village now-have been used for lifting subsoil water.

By the large, cultivators still use bullocks and wooden ploughs for tilling the land. Since a few years, however, a multi-purpose powertiller has been available in the village, owned and operated by a group of poor villagers (see below). Weeding and threshing are still done in the traditional way.

Land and labour

From the 1960s the demand for agricultural labour has increased tremendously in Konabari. As only seven labourers are left in the village nowadays, the bulk of the workforce has to be recruited from outside. Most of the migrant labourers, who work for individual wages, come from scarcity areas in Mymensingh District. Though some of them may have a contract with a specific Konabari landowner, most of them stand waiting at the local bus stop in the early morning to be hired for the day. During one of the rather frequent agricultural peaks their daily income may be as high as *taka* 35/- plus three meals, but in slack periods this goes down to *taka* 10/- plus three meals.

Sharecropping is common in the village, Under the prevailing conditions the sharecropper provides all the inputs and the harvest is shared on a fifty/fifty basis. Another quite common way of getting access to land is mortgage. There are two types. One of these, also prevailing elsewhere in Bangladesh, implies use of the land for a stipulated time against provision of a certain sum of money. The land goes back to the owner when the contract period has expired. If the owner wants to recover the use of his land before this point in time, however, he can do so against payment of an amount which equals the original sum depreciated on the basis of time passed. The other type of mortgage has no time limit. The use of the land will only return to its owner when he is able to pay back the original loan.

Village politics

The immigration of a large group of Muslims after Partition had strong political repercussions. The new-comers formed a village majority, led by Mr. Alim. The Muslims who already lived in Konabari, hitherto a minority in essentially a Hindu village, aligned them-selves against the immigrants under the leadership of Mr. Masud, taking support from a neighbouring village. Accordingly the foundation was laid for the two faction pattern which has prevailed untill now.

In the newcomers' faction a three leaders' core emerged in course of time. Mr. Alim however, remained most prominent. He was, for instance, instrumental in getting the first government sponsored shallow tubewell in the village. The other two leaders are, like Mr. Alim, rich landowners, one of whom regularly receives money from his son in the USA. All three have personal relations with administrative officers and regional politi-cians, which enables them to act as brokers for their clientele. Moreover, as rich landowners they are able to provide access to land, labour opportunities and loans to their followers. Recently Mr. Alim, an old man by now, gained access to a new asset. In early 1986 he became the manager for Konabari of the loan-providing scheme of a small international NGDO. The possibility to provide loans upto *taka* 1000/- to the local poor provides him with an additional means of patronage.

In the other faction a slightly different pattern can be observed. Mr. Masud faded to the background when he was jailed after supporting the Pakistan army during the Liberation War. His role was then taken on by his son, Mr. Fazil, an extremely resourceful man with an agressive style of politics. Mr. Masud had already given a firm footing to his leadership by getting himself elected a Basic Democrat in 1964. This enabled him to influence distribution of relief goods and of Food for Work activities. Mr. Fazil also secured an institutional political position by being elected an Union *Parishad* member in 1983. Already in the 1980 *Gram Sarkar* elections, when both Mr. Alim and Mr. Fazil contested, it had become evident that most villagers, including immigrants, rallied behind the much younger Mr. Fazil. By that time he had already impressed the villagers by installing a rival shallow tubewell and, through a strong political move, taking over supervision of the tubewell Mr. Alim had installed years ago. In this way he managed to become the sole waterlord of Konabari. In addition, from his newly gained Union *parishad* position he has access to many external resources. So, he has provided some poor villagers with ration cards and secured a road construction Food for Work Project.

He has also strong ties with the present nationally leading Jatio party and probably has wider than just local political ambitions.

The political process in Konabari has increasingly become determined by control of access to resources outside the village. Internal resources like provision of land in sharecropping, wage laour and loans have become less important. This is both an indication and a consequence of the village's increasing incorporation in wider economic and political structures. The provision of economic security and possibilities to engage in economic activities via loans provided by an outside agency we shall call the Bank is, in fact, part of this process.

Development activities

As far as the local poor are concerned development activities in the village-apart from Food for Work labour opportunities and from the recent loans-scheme which is run via Mr. Alim–are carried out by the people themselves with strong support from the Bank. How this is done and what is the development philosophy behind the Bank's operations will be discussed later.

The Control Village

General

Radhapur (see map—5), situated near the river Bangshi, at six kms. from Konabari and six kms. from Madhupur, is and has always been a Muslim village. It is a relatively young village, which means that it was established over the last 100 years by immigrants from the former greater Mymensingh District. Radhapur differs significantly from the other three village we discussed as far as the position of the women is concerned. The women are kept secluded and many of them never travel outside Radhapur, except to their home village. Most women are not even allowed to visit other parts of the village. When they travel by cart or rickshaw, they are screened off by a piece of cloth. This pattern does, however, not apply to the ten women of category A. They work as servants in other people's houses, or assist them with sewing clothes and processing paddy. They can move around rather freely.

Compared to the surrounding village, Radhapur is like an island as far as its religious conservatism and the secluded position of its women are concerned. The Bank tried several times to introduce its activities, but the Radhapur men thought it too threatening a proposition and refused to cooperate.

Population

With a population of 594 people constituting 123 households Radhapur is slightly larger than Konabari. The male/female ratio at the time of the census was 98, with the men numbering 294 and the women 300. The under fifteens amount to 46.0% of the village population. A proportion of 77.2% of the heads of households and 82.5% of the adult women did not receive any formal education. The economic categorization can be seen in Table 3.1.

Agriculture, land and labour

What we said about these matters in the section on

Konabari largely also applies here. Still, there are some differences. Traditionally, cultivation of vegetables has, for instance, been more important in Radhapur. Vegetables are looked upon as cash crop and even minor cultivators use part of their land as a vegetable garden. Further, Radhapur land is irrigated by three shallow tubewells–one BRDB sponsored, two privately owned–and two deep tubewells. The latter, which are sponsored by BRDB, are meant to provide water to a few villages and are situated at Radhapur border. Presently they are under the control of leaders from neighbouring villages. This occasionally causes Radhapur cultivators a lot of hardship, as happened last year when non-availability of water ruined their wheat crop.

Though there are about 30 wage labourers in the village who regularly work in agriculture, during peak periods immigrant labourers dominate the scene. Recruitment of resident labourers is mainly done on the basis of kinship relations and *samaj* membership.

Village politics

Basically, Radhapur politics are contests between three local factions, each rooted in a patrilineage (*gusti*). One of the three dominates the political scene, due to ownership of half the village land and some outside land in addition to that. Conflicts between the factions centre around use of *khas* land and provision of irrigation water. The deep tubewell situation has, however, enlarged the political arena to three villages and, consequently, to more parties than just three. Confrontations between an outside party and the strongest Radhapur faction, whose control of a deep tubewell has been taken away in the process, have been violent. The other two Radhapur factions have aligned themselves with factions in the neighbouring villages.

Compared to Konabari, Radhapur society is still structured in a more traditional way. Cultivation is the major source of income and many villagers make a living as agricultural labourer or sharecropper. Provision of access to work, land and credit by the village elite are major political binding elements which operate against a background of relations of kinship and *samaj* membership. The five *samaj* in the village have a strong control over people's lives. Decisions on marriages and on whom to vote for in elections are made there. Still, new organizational forms cross-cut both faction and *samaj*. Members of the BRDB cooperative and of the two local credit associations come from different factions and lineages.

Development activities

As in Konabari, the local BRDB cooperative only includes more well-to-do cultivators. The local poor do, however, participate in the two (unregistered) village credit associations (*palli samity*). These associations have operated now since three to four years. They are meant to expire after five years. Then the spoils will be divided and a new *samity* set up. Each of the funds collects a small amount—one or two *taka*—from each member weekly. Originally, they began with giving out loans on interest but without collateral, but they changed this policy due to the collection problems they faced. Now both funds concentrate on mortgaging, while some of their capital is used to provide loans to members. One *samity* has 35 members, ten of whom are women. When we asked them about their membership the women told us to have joined the *samity* in order to safeguard their earnings from spending by their husbands. Most members of this association economically belong to A and B category households. The other association has 24 members with approximately the same economic background. There are no female members.

THE BANK

The Bank has a hierarchical organization and offices, like every bank. It distinguishes itself because its staff members visit the clients in their village. Moreover, because these clients form a clearly delineated category. The Bank's target-group are the landless, defined as families owning less than 0.5 acre of cultivable land and whose total assets do not exceed the value of one acre of medium quality land. The basic assumption from which the Bank works is that the millions of landless rural people in Bangladesh, who are presently under-employed or without labour possibilities, could become productive if they got access to cheap financial resources. When supplied with loans on reasonable conditions they will engage in self-employment in fields like transport, post-harvest operations, trade and marketing. Besides, providing women with credit and, as such, enabling them to become an earning household member, will enhance their status in society.

The Bank, established as a scheduled bank in 1983, emerged from a banking project. This had the additional objectives to eliminate exploitation by money lenders and to provide an organizational format to the rural poor, as well as a basis of socio-political and economic strength through mutual support. Hence, besides the individual loans also group loans for collective economic endeavours are provided. Moreover, each group operates a group fund and an emergency fund, both based on savings by its members. The first fund is meant for consumptive lending by members, e.g. for wedding expenses. The second fund has more of an insurance character. Members can draw from it in time of need, e.g. when death or illness has struck.

The Bank works according to strict principles, emphasizing regularity of meetings and repayments. A strong principle all bank workers were found to adhere to in their conduct is to keep aloof from the local and regional elite. Each village is visited weekly by two bank employees, one for the male and one for the female groups. Motivation, basic accounting skills and the modus operandi of the Bank are transferred during introductory courses and refresher workshops. The chairpersons–there are a male and a female chairperson in each village—have a general workshop each year, where they discuss a specific issue.

In the 1984 female chairpersons' meeting a 16 points resolution was passed which stresses a certain conduct all group members should adhere to. The resolution emphasizes : house improvement and repair, kitchen gardening, education of children, bodily and environmental cleanliness, building and use of a pit latrine, drinking of tubewell or boiled water, not to give or take dowry, abolishing child marriage, collective action and mutual support. During weekly group meetings and other sessions these principles are recited and discussed.

In fact, with the 16 points resolution the Bank's programme has gained an additional "awareness raising" element. It is, however, rather specific and action-oriented. As such, it differs considerably from a conscientization approach. This would start with each group again from an inventory and analysis of problems poor people are facing. Consequently, it would use this to educate them and to make them take action, mainly directed at removing or mitigating the causes of the problems. Usually, though not necessarily, there would be some emphasis on actions geared towards getting more access to economic resources at the local level.

2. The Economic Position

This section focuses on the effects of participation in activities of the Bank for the economic position of poor households. After the presentation of some economic profiles of village household, a number of general issues with indicator value touched upon in these cases will be discussed in more detail.

Case no. 13 . *the trader-cum-tractor driver*

Karim, category A, in his mid-forties, actively

participates in Bank activities. He took four loans for trading purposes. He is married and has three young daughters. His wife is one of the female *mahajan* in the village. His elder sister and her ailing husband live in the same compound. Karim and his family inhabit a one room house, to which he recently added a C. I. sheet roof. His income comes partly from trading : presently he sells fruit *sherbet* in Modhupur *bazaar*. Additionally, he operates the male group's multipurpose powertiller, which during peak seasons brings in *taka* 30/-, plus tips, a day. He also brings in money when selling vegetables from the kitchen garden which his wife cultivates. It is she, however, who keeps the accounts of this operation and manages the money. Moreover, she earns by selling the chickens and pigeons she raises. Though their standard of living is still modest, there recently has been some improvement. Inside the house, the most striking piece of furniture is a wooden cot, which was bought not long ago. The quantity of their meals has improved, as did the quality. Karim and his wife each have two pairs of clothes, and they spent *taka* 200/- on food and clothes at *Eid*.

Still, there are also drawbacks. Two years ago he lost money in the collective pineapple venture. At the same time he had to go to the hospital to have his ulcer treated, after which he was advised to rest. His illness cost him about *taka* 2500/-. He met these expenses by selling most of his homestead land.

Case no. 14 : *a middle-aged wage labourer*

Rahman, his wife and two sons occupy a tiny house in the homestead of a distant relative. Inside there is only the mat on which they sleep. His wife is often ill after her sterilization. His two young sons do not go to school. Their main income is the payment he receives for working on the land of others. Recently, a Bank loan gave him the opportunity to share-crop in a bit of land. They also get some money from the kitchen garden which she cultivates, while he sells the products and keeps the accounts and money. An earlier effort to use a Bank loan to become a trader misfired when he got ill. In addition to this illness and that of his wife, they also met with economic disasters, like when the wheat crop was ruined on the sharecropped land. To cover the loss he had to sell a goat, and some paddy they had in store, as well as take a loan from a relative to cover the lean period. Though they are really poor he feels there has been some improvement in the meals they presently can afford. The access to the Bank's credit has brightened the future, though his participation in the pineapple and powertiller ventures has not brought him any improvement. On the contrary, one has already brought him a loss, the other may do so too.

Vertical mobility

Keeping in mind the reservations made before about investigating vertical social mobility, the following two observations can be made. First, when comparing past and present main sources of income of our sample households, rating trade and cultivation as higher than wage labour, we must conclude that the poor of Konabari have been more upwardly mobile than those of Radhapur, Besides, in Konabari those from the sample T_1 show highest upward mobility. Five years ago ten of our sample T_1 poor households mainly earned from wage labour, now only four ; eight of sample T_2 did so, against five now ; nine of the sample T_3 against nine now. When we asked the heads of households to compare their present economic rating with that of five years' ago, the above picture was repeated (Table 3.4).

Second, when looking carefully at the economic situation of poor households we observed that this may change rather drastically and quickly. The present nine households among the Radhapur poor, are, for instance, not the same as the past nine : both upward and downward mobility took place among them. How quickly things can change we saw when doing our in depth interviews : a few households which rated A category at the time of the census, were clearly on the way up during later visits. There is, moreover, a seasonal pattern to mobility, due to the slack in agriculture (see also Chaudhury,

1981 and Clay, 1981). In Konabari the seasonality especially hits traders, however, as the market contracts for a few months each year.

The explanation for the pattern of vertical mobility in Konabari indicated above is a combination of the effects of the interventions of the Bank and the general improvement of economic conditions in the wake of agricultural modernization, which gave a boost to petty trading. When we look at the Bank's operations, we observe that about half of the heads of poor households in Konabari and just under a quarter of the adult women from those households, have been taking loans from the Bank (Tables 3.7 and 3.8). This money was largely invested in trading and cultivation.

As to trading we have observed that the loans obtained from the Bank are both much larger and cheaper than those from *mahajan*. Further, we found that trading is done more as a constant operation, as compared to its intermittent nature when credit is hard to get, as is presently the case among small-traders in sample T_2. Moreover, the geographical mobility of Konabari traders proved to be high ; they now cover *haat* in neighbouring villages and in Mòdhupur town. Among the Konabari poor who did not join a credit group upward mobility is less, because of lesser access to cheap and sizeable credit. Still, those who managed to get involved in trading also began to move around more widely and also benefitted from an increasing demand,

Although the poor of Radhapur could have benefitted from the expanding economy as well, their village's cultural code prevented them from taking advantage. There, trade is rated lower than agricultural work, and female mobility is nearly absent. Loans from *mahajan* were largely used for covering disaster spending. Still, we met poor Radhapur women who ached to begin a trading business, willing to break the behavioural norms. But they found cheap and sizeable credit to be unavailable to them.

Our remarks about suddenness, speed and reversibility of vertical mobility can best be elucidated by some case material.

Case no. 15 : *an enterprising woman*

Aziza (aged 40, category B) works in the village rice mill as a labourer and is paid in kind. She took some Bank loans and bought two rickshaws which she hires out to her sons on a daily basis. Her husband left her some time ago to stay with his second wife, where she had to start fully supporting herself and her family. We expect that she will rate as a category C household in the near future.

Case no. 16 : *two downward mobile men*

I

Hannan is considered to be the poorest man in the village, though once he was a well-to-do farmer. Nowadays he is a wage labourer, reduced to a dilapidated house, where he lives with his wife and children. Some time ago he joined a Bank group and got a loan, but he did not succeed in investing it profitably. Instead, he incurred heavy losses. Now people point at him as an example of a good-for-nothing.

II

When taking the census in November 1985, we met Enayat, a hotel owner rating C category. During the first half of 1986 we saw his business go down hill and neighbours informed us that he had become addicted to the movies, spending much money and not doing any work. When we left he worked as a labourer in the local rice mill.

Income

In Konabari trading is currently the main source of income both of poor households and in the village as a whole. In Radhapur poor households are primarily earning by wage labour, with cultivation, especially of share-cropped and mortgaged in land, coming in second place. If we take the village Radhapur as a whole, then cultivation is the primary source of income (Table 3.2). When considering such information, we have to take into account, that the total income of poor households is a conglomerate of various sources. In this respect the poor of all three samples did not show any difference.

In all three samples we found women earning an income

even proportionally more so in T_3 than in T_1 sample. They raise poultry, grow vegetables, husk paddy. Besides, in Konabari they are, as we already saw, engaged in business, while also some of them (four) work in the ricemill or even (at least three) operate as moneylender. Working women are often paid in kind ; as is the case with those working in the ricemill, for instance, whose male colleagues are paid in cash.

Standard of living

Cultivable land is the most coveted resource, but in Konabari 34 out of 72 heads of households did not own any of it, as compared to 48 out of 123 in Radhapur. At the top of the scale in Radhapur we found 15 heads of households owning more than 200 decimals, as to ten in Konabari, while five out of these ten owned more than 500 decimals. Assuming that both sets of figures are equally reliable, they point at slightly more concentration of land-ownership in Konabari.

Ownership of agricultural implements is clearly most prevalent in the various B Category households in both villages. There is, further, a conspicuous lack of implements among the A category households of Konabari, as compared to those of Radhapur, corresponding, of course, with the difference in their main source of income. Poor households in Radhapur also slightly more often owned cows. In both villages goats were sometimes kept on sharecropping basis. Raising poultry is common among all the poor.

As regards food, we are not really able to draw solid conclusions beyond the statement that many respondents deemed their meals bigger though certainly not better than before. If there is an improvement it implies replacement of wheat by rice, some more fish and milk and sometimes even meat. A lesser extent of poverty is usually not expressed in the clothes people wear. Only in C and D categories do people spend still relatively large amounts on clothes when they already have some which they can wear. The poor do differently. When they have earned beyond their immediate needs, they reinvest, pay off debts, improve their houses. We found several households where mothers and daughters, fathers and sons owned one good *sari* or *lungi*, and between them shared one more to bathe in, even if they could afford to buy another. And if they buy, for instance on the occasion of *Eid* or *Puja*, it often is a used one.

Giving or taking dowry at weddings is highly prevalent in both villages. Over the last five years 42 marriages took place in all our sample households together. At 26 (61.9%) of these occasions dowry was provided. Taking the samples separately, we observed that among sample T_1 weddings the percentage is nearest to that just mentioned (63.2%) ; in sample T_2 it is slightly less (50%) and in sample T_3 slightly more (72.7%). Dowry may be given in both kind and cash and its value may run into thousands of *taka*. We did not actually screen which resource people used for making such big amounts available. Still one case we came across may be mentioned, not so much because it is indicative, but more for its exceptionality.

Case no. 17 : *compilation of a dowry*

Suniti, the second daughter of Rakhal is a Bank group member as is her father. When she was married in 1984 her dowry amounted to *taka* 6000/-. Besides her father had to face marriage expenses of *taka* 4000/-. To get the money together some of Suniti's savings from trading business were used, while her father borrowed from the group fund. Additionally they got a *taka* five contribution from all the female and three quarters of the male group members in the village.

Indebtedness

In both villages poor households are indebted nearly all and certainly most of the time. They incur debts to meet disaster spending, to buy clothes or pay a dowry, to make both ends meet in lean periods, and to secure a livelihood or finance an endeavour to improve their economic basis. What is new and different between the villages, is the increase of credit sources in Konabari, a high incidence there of using loans for productive purposes, and a lesser dependence on traditional local Konabari *mahajan*.

The poor in Konabari may take large loans from the Bank or the recently introduced credit scheme run by Mr. Alim for, respectively, 16% or 10% a year. As compared to this, informal sources may want as much as 20% a month. Such informal sources may be other poor, who set up small business as a moneylender. We met three women, not members of a Bank-group, who earned an income in this way, using money they had accumulated by petty trading. We also came across three Bank-group members, a man and two women, who used part of their Bank loan as moneylending capital. Actually, the number of poor actively engaged in commercial moneylending may be higher than this, as the stigma attached to the activity makes it a difficult subject to investigate.

Relatives are also important sources of credit to the poor ; they may or may not ask interest, depending on the size and the duration of the transaction. In-laws usually do not, in order to prevent conflict between husband and wife because of it. Then there are the wholesalers (betelnut, vegetables, fruit) in Modhupur *bazaar*, who have taken on the role of the Konabari elite as *mahajan*. We were often told by our respondents that these wholesalers treat them with deference and are quite willing to supply a loan. This may well be related to the poor's present somewhat firmer economic basis and, of course, to their link with the Bank.

In Radhapur, the situation has hardly changed at all. Moneylending is limited to the categories of well-to-do villagers, relatives, and, the odd poor moneylender, like the one woman we met among our sample's ladies. The two private funds do not prove to be an extra source of credit, but focus on earning money for their members through a mortgaging business. Finally, two observations with regard to moneylending in both villages. First, loans are commonly paid off with other loans from other sources. In Konabari, part of Bank loans are also used in this respect. Second, timely repayment of loans is tried at all costs, mainly in order to maintain the moneylender's confidence. As to repayment of Bank loans and those of relatives, social control pays an additional pressurizing role.

Savings

If we use the folk notion of savings prevailing in both villages, i. e. savings as the accumulation of a large sum of money, our respondents hardly save at all. Still, when we see savings in terms of delayed consumption, saving is done almost continuously among the poor. Women raise poultry and grow vegetables ; they may take a handful of rice from every meal to store for a rainy day, or to meet the regular expenses of their daughter's education at the village religious school. Though they do not consider livestock as savings, cows and goats may come in handy when in dire straits. There is, of course, also the rather compulsory formal saving, like the group tax of the Bank, and the requirements of the private credit funds in Radhapur.

Economic vulnerability

Both domestic and economic disasters are common visitors among the poor. It greatly contributes to keeping them in a near constant condition of indebtedness. Obviously, high incidence of disease and death is to be expected, as the poor live under adverse conditions of insufficient diet, bad hygiene, bad housing. Additionally, proper treatment of diseases at an early stage may be delayed as funds are short, often leading to a more serious and, usually, costly situation. Delay or lack of cure because of insufficient treatment, may also drain resources over a longer period of time.

Economic disasters, like floods, droughts, blight, dead livestock, or the misfiring of a collective Bank project, are the other category of calamity.

Usually disaster expenditure is covered by a variety of resources, loans from *mahajan* and kin figuring prominently among them. It struck us that the Bank's emergency fund and group fund, both meant to be of help in this kind of occasion, were hardly drawn upon. The probable reason for this is that both funds can only be drawn from by one member at a time. Only after repayment of such a loan, the next member can borrow. Besides, we were informed that when sometimes money is needed really urgently, usually when illness strikes, access to the funds requires too much of a hassle.

Case no. 18 : ***costs of disasters and how they are met***

I

> Rakhal, category B, is a trader using a Bank loan. When his father died he spent *taka* 5000/- on funeral and ritual expenses, for which he borrowed from the Bank and from his relatives. The ritual required him not to work for a month. Subsequently he fell ill and had to have an operation. The costs of this he covered with the loan from a *mahajan*, who

charged 50% interest over six months. He had to rest some weeks before he could start earning again. Months later when we met him he had not yet paid off the *mahajan*. The Bank loan he did pay from his wife's income as a trader. But this was not sufficient and he had been forced to take another moneylender's loan.

II

Alfat is an A category Bank-group member. He is wage labourer, but sharecrops on the side. Two years ago his crop was badly damaged which ultimately forced him to take a loan of *taka* 1000/-against 20% interest a month. In addition a pickpocket robbed him off his *taka* 1000/- Bank loan money. He overcame this new loss only with great difficulty and tightening of his belt, but managed to stay clear from taking yet another loan.

III

Amzad, category B, earns by cultivating and trading both, using Bank loans. His 16 year old son Sultan helps him. Last April Sultan fell severely ill with tetanus and both an allopathic practitioner and a folk healer were called to treat him. The treatment cost him hundreds of *taka*, while he also had to abstain from work for a while. To meet expenses he sold a cow and two *maund* of paddy, besides taking loans from *mahajan* and relatives. Several neighbours and relatives also provided small amounts of paddy on the basis of mutuality. Sultan was saved.

3. The Political Situation in the Villages

As we saw in an earlier section, village politics in Konabari and Radhapur are factional in character, but still rather different. Although regional macro-economic changes had an impact in both the villages, their impact was more drastic in Konabari, where the introduction of the Bank's activities further contributed to the changes. In this village many of the poor have become less dependent on local patrons as they primarily became entrepreneurs with access to outside credit resources. To acquire land to till they still of course must turn to the landowners. Radhapur society changed as well, but far less dramatically, and local patronage retained much of its importance. Moreover, in this village the *samaj* still play a strong political role, even if some new alignments do now cross-cut their membership.

We shall now investigate political changes which occurred in more detail, focussing on interactions between poor and more well-to-do villagers, labour conditions, and voting behaviour of the poor.

How poor and elite treat and see each other

As many poor have left agriculture, at least temporarily, and usually do not approach the elite for credit, interactions between them have gradually diminished. One of the village leaders expressed this clearly : "nowadays they (the poor) seem too busy and as a result have little time to talk to me. They used to visit me often and spend hours in my house. Now they have no time to come, even if I send for them." Another remark which we often heard was that agricultural wage demands had risen since the arrival of the Bank.

In both villages, none of the poor has any good words for the elite. They consider them leeches, always on the move to rob the poor off what little land they may have left. We were often told by them, when referring to the village *matabar* : "they will never be our friends." In Radhapur, the poor treat the elite with deference ; in Konabari, generally with both disregard and deference, which reflects that they are still dependent, but less so.

Case no. 19 : *disregard and deference in Konabari*

I

Torab, then present Union *Parishad* member's elder brother one day was loudly threatening to kill Rahim's goat because of its alleged damaging of his crop. Rahim's wife (A category) and some other poor women stood nearby, but hardly even looked at him and carried on as though nothing happened. He left muttering to himself, without taking any further action.

II

Joy (categoryA), house servant, once was severely beaten up by his master Kalim (category D). This enraged Joy's brothers who, in their turn, beat up Kalim. Soon afterwards the brothers realized they might have made a mistake as Kalim had provided all of them with work over the years. During a *salish* they publicly apologized to Kalim. In general, the village poor did not clearly support them in this case.

III

One day we stood talking to a poor villager. A well-to-do land owner passed us on the road and we greeted him. Directly, afterwards our talking partner said, "Why are you greeting these people ? They are leeches !"

Clear examples of individual or joint resistance are rare in both the villages. The aforementioned beating case is one of them. In Radhapur we found another individual case, of a servant who walked out on his master after having been abused badly. He did not return, and left the wealthy landowner to till his own land. Cases like these may well indicate a lower level of tolerance among the poor of abusive behaviour. Lack of supportive material makes it impossible, however, to decide whether we are dealing here with a trend.

Collective resistance is rare ; when asking around among our sample respondents, we found two cases only, both in Konabari,

Case no. 20 : *collective opposition in Konabari*

I

A few years back a rich farmer from a neighbouring village slapped Amir Ali the then village Bank-group Chairman during a row. Subsequently, the deputy chairman mobilized all the male members. They grabbed the farmer's brother and kept him hostage till a suitable apology had been made during a *salish*.

II

Rearing goats has always been an important subsidiary source of income of the poor. At about the same time as the above case happened, the village elite jointly decided to ban rearing of goats in the village, as these animals allegedly destroyed their crops. This time virtually all the village poor unitedly opposed the decision and carried on keeping their goats.

Labour relations

Changes in agricultural conditions have led to changes in labour relations in both villages. Nowadays there are more and shorter cropping cycles than before. Cultivation has become more labour intensive than it used to be. The villagers themselves refer to changes by saying that the number of *jo*, i.e., the prime time for an agricultural activity, have become more, while at the same time their lengths have shortened much.

Such developments have increased the demand for labour.

In addition, shortening of the *jo* made traditional forms of labour exchange between cultivators uneconomical. They now were forced to call in outside labour where previously a neighbour or a relative would have helped them out. When in Konabari the number of local wage labourers decreased, due to a conversion to other sources of income, the rising demand for labour was met by migrant labourers.

Together, the increasing demand and the decreasing number of local labourers put, of course, upward pressure on the wages. Hence, the relative bargaining power of each individual wage labourer who works in Konabari has increased. This is regardless whether he lives in the village or comes in by bus. Migrant labourers when haggling with potential employers at the bus stand try to use this power individually. The larger influx of migrants has, however, led to a supply situation where the few remaining local labourers in Konabari cannot really cash in on their relative scarcity. They often expressed this resentfully to us follows : "If the migrants would not have come, our earning might well have been *taka* 100/- a day." Now they may run up to *taka* 35/- plus three meals. These meals are, incidentally, not what they used to be. Each labourer we met expressed the opinion that the landowners had purposefully economized on their quantity during the last few years.

The last statement may well reflect that Konabari landowners on the whole have become more oriented towards capitalist farming. The observation is at least supported by the fact that prevalence of share cropping seems to be falling. We were told by some of our respondents who would like to take up the tilling of the land again, but now as a sharecropper instead of a labourer, that acquiring land for share-cropping was really hard. According to them the landowners were more inclined to cultivate their land themselves, with the help of wage labourers.

The above developments, are largely, also to be observed in Radhapur. Labour relations have been changing there as well. But, like we explained before, wage labour has there, as yet, retained its importance as a source of income for the poor. Besides, we have observed a higher prevalence of sharecropping among the poor.

Voting behaviour

In both villages the poor vote according to their factional alignment. In Konabari the elections of 1980 and 1983 gave the young leader Mr. Fazil the opportunity to, respectively, gauge the extent of his support and establish himself as the real big man of the village. The votes of most of the poor supported him at these occasions. The women we interviewed reported to have voted according to their husbands instructions. In Radhapur the poor did vote according to their *samaj* decision. Most of the women did not vote, as was the wish of the *samaj*. Only a few poor women cast their vote and consequently were looked down upon by other villagers.

In neither village did the poor vote for anybody from their own class, though at the 1983 Union *Parishad* elections there was an opportunity to do so. Muslim Miah, a member of a Bank-group in a nearby village contested, but he lost. His fellow-poor from Konabari and Radhapur did not support him (see also Siddiqui, 1984:31). They told us, when referring to this case, that a poor man will never make a good leader, as he is not able to rise above his own needs. He is too busy looking after his own interest. In this way they explained that their decision not to vote for him was, indeed, a sensible one.

4. The Position of the Women

Case no. 21 : *two poor women's lives*

I

Rahima (A category, aged 23) is the wife of a wage labour. She has three young children, two daughters and a son. The household lives in a small thatch roofed house in an extended family compound. At dawn she begins her day by letting her hens out of the chicken house and feeding them. Then she sweeps the house and prepares breakfast. She cooks on a stove using fuel which she has to collect during the day. After breakfast she washes utensils and cutlery and fetches water from a tube-well a hundred yards away. She does the laundry, cleans the house, attends to her kitchen garden. At harvest time, in addition she will dry, parboil, again dry and, consequently, husk and winnow the paddy, using the husks as fuel. She also prepares rice cakes at each harvesting time, and prepares puffed rice for the children. Sometimes she goes to a jute field to collect some leaves to be used as green vegetables. In the afternoon she takes her children for a bath in the river, taking lunch after returning home. If she is not busy with post-harvest operations, she may repair some clothes. Around sunset she starts preparing the meal, using some vegetables and, sometimes fish, her husband has brought home. Then the whole family eats together. Most important family matters are decided on by Rahima and her husband together. She was encouraged to become a group member by her husband, who participates in the Bank's activities himself as well. Together they will decide on taking loans and on their utilization. They also decided together to educate their children and, accordingly, recently sent their eldest daughter to school. Buying small household items, like soap and oil, Rahima does herself when vendors come round to the house. Large purchases, such as food and clothes, are made by her husband in the *bazaar*. Rahima can move freely around in the village, but preferably so in her own *para*. She feels that such mobility has increased since the Bank has arrived. She is confident that, when the occasion arrives, her daughter's wedding will be openly discussed with her and her opinion taken into account.

II

Aziza (category B, aged 40) is a labourer in the local ricemill. Previously she was the women groups' chairwoman. Three sons and a daughter are living with her. Her husband left, to live with his second wife. He visits them, but does not give any financial support. So the and her sons have to support the household. They live in a C. I sheet roofed house on her mother's brother's land. She has sunk a tubewell and installed a pit latrine, reflecting her previous status as pioneering chairwoman. At dawn she rises and prepares the breakfast, which is followed by feeding ducks, hens and goats. Next she cleans the house and feeds the children. Then it is time to go to the ricemill, where she stays on for nine hours, with a brief break for lunch and bath. During this break, or after ricemill work, she has to wash the clothes, collect firewood and attend to the animals. The children usually give a helping hand. During the day she also has to go to the Bank to get loans. After sunset she begins to prepare the meal. Living alone, she decides everything by herself. She is, however, not beyond asking advice from her brother and/or her mother. When marrying off her daughter last year Aziza did all the negotiations herself, her brother helping her out when needed. Aziza has always been working outside, but since the arrival of the Bank she has become more mobile, even attending a workshop in a town 160 kms. away. She also goes to the Modhupur cinema. Shopping outside the village she still considers out of bounds. For this she depends on her brother and her sons.

Economic decision-making

In both villages women bring in an income, usually in kind, from working in other houses or, in Konabari, in the ricemill. Moreover, most women earn an income through raising poultry, rearing goats, growing vegetables, processing of agricultural products for others or for sale.

Such income earning work is largely perceived as an extension of women's normal household duties. The income earned is either directly consumed (if in kind) stored for a while, or used for everyday household expenses. Depending on how it has been earned, some may be reinvested or recycled into the moneylending or trading business. Women usually have a large say in the spending of the income they bring in, though the possible ways to spend (broken) rice and small amounts of cash are, of course, limited. Additionally, they are not supposed to visit the *bazaar*.

The three female moneylenders and some female traders had acquired much room to manoeuvre in their business. One of the husbands even referred to his wife's moneylending as "her department", indicating that he did not want to have a say there.

Women have little or no control of the way their husband's income is spent. Major economic decisions are still the realm of the man, who may or may not consult his wife. Some husbands only mention important purchases after they have been made.

With regard to borrowing money, women are supposed to decide independently on small amounts, like *taka* ten to twenty, and household items, like small quantities of rice, vegetables or salt. Most men believe however, that women are not able to handle big amounts of money, whence they do not let them. Loans from the Bank are usually taken by women after consultation with their husband or son who are then also consulted on the utilization of the money.

Besides the leeway that has been obtained by the female moneylenders and some female traders regarding the running of their business, we did not find much difference between the villages as to women's influence on economic decision-making.

Decisions on marriage and education

Only with regard to their daughter's marriage is the opinion of women considered important in both village societies. Still, in Radhapur, in general, the *samaj* largely decides on marriages and women's voice does not count there. This difference between villages could not be observed with regard to the brides to be : they have no say, unless it is their second marriage.

Though usually husband and wife decide on

educational matters together in both villages, this statement needs more precision in order to better reflect the actual situation. It must be realized that many of the women did not have any education themselves and, therefore can hardly gauge the importance of sending their children to school. Additionally, the poorest households are hardly able to afford the clothes, books, and and fees required. With respect to the education of girls we found, further, a remarkable difference between Konabari and Radhapur. In the last villages girls usually only receive religious education ; those who go to primary school form the exception there. In Konabari on the contrary, girls were encouraged to go to primary school.

General treatment of women

In both the villages the general picture regarding women's treatment is the same. They eat at rather irregular times, especially during a busy harvest period. The Muslim women may eat with their husbands and children at night but then will serve them first, giving them the best portions. In lean periods they may sometimes only take some puffed rice, or hardly anything at all. Wife beating and abusing is common in both places, but more so in the early days and years of the marriage, especially before a child has been born. By and large, women regard men as unfaithful and they often said : "one cannot trust a man". Almost one third of the women in both the villages showed a strong fear of their husbands taking subsequent wives, with or without divorcing them first.

Mobility

Following the introduction of Bank activities the physical mobility of women in Konabari has considerably increased. They attend meetings, participate in trainings and workshops and have to draw loans from the Bank office outside the village. Many of them also rather often visit the movie theatre in Modhupur. The enhanced physical mobility, also inside the village, applies to both Bank-group members and other women. There is, it seems, a positive inclination in Konabari society towards mobility and independence of the women. We came across only few a men who made a negative remark on the issue, when asked to comment on it.

The situation in Radhapur is a great contrast. There the women's mobility is much restricted ; the common notion is that women should not move around too much, and many men and women even prefer them to stay between four walls as much as possible.

The several poor women who work as house maids, did vote at election time and even form the nuclei of groups, stand out conspicuously. They are looked down upon but it does not seem to hurt them. Indeed, they truly have "nothing left to loose", which makes them appear rather invulnerable.

5. The Organization of the Poor

The subject of this section is the extent to which the poor have become organized on the basis of their socio-economic position. The discussion will focus particularly on the prevalence and structure of collective actions and on feelings of solidarity among the poor.

Organization at Village-level and Above

The major change as to the poor's organization has been, of course, the arrrival of the Bank. Hence, we shall start our review there.

In March 1980 the Bank began to operate in Konabari. As elsewhere, five member male and female groups were established. In May 1980 four male groups were formed followed by an additional four in August 1981. Two female groups came into being in March 1981, two more in August 1982, and the last one in March 1983. On the whole, group membership has been stable. Only one man was replaced due to insolvency in the initial period, while presently two female members are 'dormant' for the same reason. Until 1985 Konabari was one of the Bank's best villages in the region in terms of savings and repayment. Since then, its record has deteriorated.

In fact, the Bank-groups, their village-level chairpersonship and the meetings during workshops and training form the major organizational platform of the Konabari poor. The hawkers association set up by male hawkers in the Modhupur Bazaar in 1985 might, however, also offer a bright organizational prospect. Its objective is to further the petty traders interest by regulating their trading operations. Members are allocated a place in the *bazaar* and what they should sell is decided after negotiations in the committee. The 30 members which the committee consisted of when we left paid one *taka* as weekly contribution. Two men from Konabari had joined the committee, one was a Bank group member as well. He was in fact, the hawkers association's Secretary.

In Radhapur, the situation is very much different. In this village there are no lines to the poor of other villages, besides, of course, primordial ties. Still, in the village itself, the two *palli samity* form a feeble organizational beginning, as may the small groups set up by some women who do eagerly want the Bank to come in. They managed to organize three such groups, but the Bank requires five before starting its activities. As yet, the credit funds do not go beyond their economic aim and the small female groups in their formation phase may well wither away if they are not given a content of activity.

Views of the Bank

In Konabari most of the poor, whether participating in its activities or not, are positive about the Bank. Group-members point at their reduced economic vulnerability and at the opportunity they got to choose another source of income than agricultural labour, which might have crippled them before long. The large majority of members mentioned economic objectives as their main reason to join a group. They see the Bank primarily as an additional source of credit. Their major commitment is to improve their own household's economic status. Like Karim said "when I am prosperous I shall discontinue my group membership of course".

Yet, we also heard some grudges, especially about the

recent tightening of Bank rules regarding defaulting. Such members remarked that "now the Bank's stomach is full, it does not care about its members anymore". Some of the non-participants in Bank activities explained their negative view by pointing their finger at cases of poor who had lost in collective endeavours, or who had to take expensive *mahajan* loans or sell some land to cover repayment of a Bank loan.

By and large, the poor of Radhapur are rather indifferent about the Bank, most women do not even seem to know of its existence. Therefore, the group forming activity of some poor women, we already referred to this several times before, is the more astonishing. To put their efforts in proper perspective, we have to remind ourselves that access to sufficient cheap credit for such enterprising women is virtually nil in the village where they live.

Collective economic action

In 1983 the male Bank groups in Konabari jointly took up cultivation of a leased pineapple garden, using a joint Bank loan for the purpose. Cultivation was done by some members against payment of the usual wage, while the then *kendra prodhan* managed the operation. Due to a poor harvest and lack of management experience the enterprise misfired. It ended in a loss of *taka* 5000/-, to be paid by the members. When we left they still had to pay back half of this debt.

After this negative experience, there was still eagerness to try again, although the nature of the next joint activity was heavily disputed. Finally, it was decided to buy a multi-purpose powertiller using a loan of *taka* 91.000/-. This time only 30 out of 40 male group members participated, though quite a few did so grudgingly, as instead they would have preferred to install a shallow tubewell. They told us that they more or less had been forced to provide their signature to the loan request, and that some signatures even had been forged. They see the endeavour as a burden which eventually will tie them down for many years with payment of interest and installments, before there will be any gain for them. As yet, the powertiller has not been a success. Twice it broke down and had to be taken to Dhaka for repair. Though it is used rather often in Konabari, its full potential has not been realized.

At the end of 1985 two Konabari male groups together took a *taka* 3000/-loan to cultivate three acres of sharecropped land with wheat. Due to the lack of rain there was a misharvest and when we left they still had to return half of the loan.

Disunity and mutuality among the poor

The initial stages of the pineapple and school (Case no. 22) endeavours were high tides of solidarity and unity among the poor of Konabari. This was clearly expressed at the occasion of Suniti's wedding when many group members came forward with financial support (case No. 16). But with the failure of the economic enterprises dissent set in. It more or less exploded shortly after the powertiller had been bought, and led to the replacement of the male groups' leadership. Though presently things seem to have returned to normal, mutual confidence among the members has not yet returned.

Among the women a change of leadership occurred as well. At the end of 1985 it was accidentally detected that the chairwoman had actually taken *taka* 1400/-out of the groupfund instead of the *taka* 400/-she had been entitled to. Though both she and her deputy were replaced, mutual confidence among the women was so badly shaken that when we left a half year later mistrust among the female members was still expressed in conversations.

Actually the tensions touched upon above could hardly have had any negative effect on mutual support among the group members. Apart from the wedding case we did not find any indication that any such support had grown beyond the already existing level of assistance between neighbours and relatives. As we saw in the tetanus case (Case no. 18) such help, though small in size, is important both financially and morally. Such mutuality seemed to be prevailing in both villages. So did exchange of labour, though at a lower level than before. An example is the repair or improvement of a house.

We did not come across any spontaneous joint economic actions, except for the *palli samity* in Radhapur. Joint fishing, joint harvesting for wages, joint paddy husking by women, and so on, did not seem to have a recent tradition in both villages.

One spontaneous collective action in another than the economic field must still be mentioned. Also in this action women did not participate.

Case no. 22 : *the rise and fall of a school*

> In mid 1985 the male Bank-group members decided to start a school for the small children of the village. The reason was the reachability problem connected with the bad location of the nearest school, namely at the other side of a busy highway.
>
> Some members contributed cash, some provided building materials and some helped to construct the building. The previous *kendra pradhan* and the present one were appointed as teachers. It was decided that the members would each pay ten *taka* towards running costs.
>
> Six months later the school hardly functioned anymore : financial contributions came irregularly as did the children. Finally the school was closed.

6. The Worldview of the Poor

Roots of Poverty

In Tangail we followed the same procedure with regard to our enquiry into people's views of causes of poverty and ways to end it, as was described in the previous chapter. The same clusters of answers could be distinguished. The distribution of answers is reported in Tables 3.10 and 3.13. Here, we shall only mention the main features of this distribution.

With respect to the causes of general poverty a fair number of respondents in all three samples had "no opinion". Further, there is remarkably little difference between the results of the three samples. In each of them "plain economic causes" score highest, with "self-accusation" in second place. In each of the samples the distribution of the answers of men and women shows most difference in the case of the "self-accusation" cluster though the nature of the difference is not the same. "Political-economic causes" score low, though highest among the women of the three samples. But the numbers are not sizeable enough to afford us drawing conclusions here. A final observation is that "fate, *karma* or the will of God" did also show a low prevalence.

As to causes of individual poverty the distribution of reactions is a bit dissimilar. First, not surprisingly, the number of "no opinion" responses is much lower. Second, "pure economic causes" and "self-accusation" again score highest, when we consider men and women jointly. If we look at them separately this pattern disappears. Third, "disasters" and "political-economic causes" do have much more response in sample T_1 than in the other two. Further, the cluster "will of God, *karma*, fate" scores highest in sample T_3, especially among the women. Finally, the distribution in both the control samples is rather similar, more so than in the case of the responses to general poverty, where men and women of the two samples hold opposite views with regard to "self-accusation".

Solutions to the poverty problem

Regarding solutions to general poverty we can see a rather high "no opinion" response in all samples, but especially in sample T_3. Further, a few respondents saw no solution and here applies what we have said about "despair" in the corresponding section of the previous chapter.

General poverty can only be solved through God's will, *karma* or fate is the opinion of many T_3 sample men and women. Still, the other two samples also show some similar responses. "Plain-economic changes" score high, especially among the women. The same applies to "self-change", though the men in sample T_3 think differently. These men score highest on "no opinion" and "fate, *karma,* and the will of God". In all three samples, but most clearly so in sample T_1, "political economic changes" have been mentioned mostly by the women. "Government action" is not expected to constitute much of a solution.

Individual poverty, so the men or women of samples T_1 and T_2 and the women of sample T_3 agree, is certainly a matter of 'self-change". The cluster "plain economic changes" is important to all samples, but less so to the men of samples T_1 and T_3. The cluster "political-economic changes" is deemed crucial mostly by the women of sample T_1, though the relatively high score among the T_3 women must also be noted. The men of the Radhapur sample are putting their faith in God's will and fate. On other solutions they, again, score comparatively low. The same pattern can be seen when we look at the men of sample T_2, though they have more faith in "self-change".

We also asked our respondents to reflect on outside assistance in finding solutions to poverty. As to the role of government in this respect the poor of the Konabari samples showed the same pattern: when reviewing the past women rated "no help" higher than "some help", while most men held the opposite view. In Radhapur most men and women agreed that they had received some government assistance.

Regarding the question what the government should do for them, a surprisingly high number of men in all three samples had "no opinion". If an opinion was viewed, creation of employment, provision of food, clothes and housing, and elimination of corruption were the tasks mentioned most often.

The role of political parties could not be defined by the respondents. Men and women of all samples neither could say what the parties had done for them, nor could they formulate a normative view towards the parties' future actions.

Views of the future

The poor of Konabari, and most clearly those participating in Bank activities, perceive their present situation as being better than that of five years ago. The majority of Radhapur respondents, on the contrary, saw no improvement (Table 3.4). This difference in perception is also present in the poor's view of the future. When we asked them to reflect on the possibility of their son (s) or grandson (s) owning more land than they did, both men and women of sample T_1 were most outspoken that this would be the case. In sample T_2, the women were rather positive about it, but the majority of men thought it a matter of fate and the will of God. In Radhapur the majority of both men and women in the sample held the same "may be or may not be" opinion, though on the whole the women were slightly more optimistic. Those who thought there would be no improvement formed a sizeable minority in all the samples.

When asked about the future of their children in more detail, education was deemed important by everybody. There was, however, a difference between men and women in all the three samples. Most men would like their sons to have higher education, e.g. a university degree, while they considered primary education to be sufficient for their daughters. The girls should then receive a complementary religious education to make them good wives and mothers.

Women, especially in Radhapur, were generally less clear about the value of children's education. Still, they emphasized primary education for the boys and religious education for the girls.

White collar jobs and business scored high (highest in sample T_1 and T_2) as future jobs for sons. Cultivation as future prospect was mentioned most often by the Radhapur sample, but it was also referred to by respondents from the two other samples, in sample T_1 almost as often as in Radhapur. Wage labourer was also mentioned as a future prospect, especially in Radhapur, where it almost reached the score of cultivation. Respondents from sample T_2 did not refer to it, but one man and one woman from sample T_1 brought it up. Finally, none of the respondents preferred a government job for their son. Still, some may have done so by implication when they mentioned "service" as a prospect.

Unity and individualism

When having discussions about the future it struck us over and over again how individually oriented our respondents were and how negative a view they held about unity among the poor. Whenever we brought up the possibility of working unitedly it was discarded. It was pointed out, instead, that disunity was common and, like jealousy and individualism, rather an inherent quality of the poor. Among them, they would say, even brothers doubted brothers, so the question of unity did not arise at all. On the one hand, they would add, a poor man cannot tolerate another poor man to prosper ; on the other hand, if a poor man gets rich, he will forget about his past and exploit his former friends. In all samples, the prevailing view was that a poor man only thinks about himself and will try to become rich at the expense of his brothers. Rahim expressed his view as follows : "it is nice and pleasing to hear about unity among the poor, but in reality I cannot trust my brother. If I give him *taka* 5000/- to invest, he shall take away both the profit and the original amount."

We got the impression that the competitive and individualist self-image of the poor has strong roots in their past, but is presently strengthened by their view of the economic situation as one of scarcity. This is probably related to their experiences of competition in trade and about land for sharecropping. For the remaining wage labourers their lower scarcity value due to the abundance of migrant labourers will play a role.

Chapter IV : Conclusion

This concluding chapter consists of two parts. First, we shall summarize the results of the study with regard to the general problem we set out from. This will be done by a separate discussion of each of the two development approaches, in which we shall consider the aspects of the position of the poor which were distinguished in the introductory chapter. After completion of this task, we continue with some reflections concerning selected features of the development approaches we have studied.

1. Results

The Emphasis on Conscientization Approach

The economic aspect

In Sunamganj we found that the economic condition of the poor who participated in the Project has, in general, not improved. The poor did largely remain poor.

In individual cases some slight changes were registered. The only additional source of income found to prevail was that of women working outside their own house or collecting and producing edible goods. The Project has been stimulating this addition by its positive influence on female mobility.

Another change which occurred was the addition of BRDB as a new source of credit for women. The women who successfully, though modestly, were drawing on this source had already been organized by the Project. This meant a clear advantage for them ; a group of women in the control village who lacked this basis did not operate effectively.

The new credit source did not change the prevailing structure of indebtedness : the poor are still regularly indebted and still mainly rely on the moneylender as a reliable source of timely and sizeable credit, though he is an extremely expensive source.

Individual savings were meagre among all poor respondents and hardly offer any protection when disaster hits. If there are savings, they are mainly used to steer through the lean period. For meeting disaster expenses all the poor go usually to the moneylender. Sale of assets is no viable strategy as these are too scarce among all of them.

Collective savings have been important to cover losses suffered as the result of class conflict. Further, they have not really been a source of much support. The present food security fund run by the women's group and meant to help them bridging the lean period, covers less than one third of the members.

The political aspect

In the project village introduction of the Project activities has changed local level politics considerably.

Though elements of factionalism can be detected now and then, the clearly prevailing structure of village politics is class conflict and polarization along class lines. Struggle for access to *khas* land and representation in positions pivotal to access to resources have been the main conflict issues, though there have been others as well.

The control village only shows isolated cases of low-key resistance by the poor, which are mainly directed at redressing what they consider as an unjust violation by the landowners of the rules governing labour relations.

Politics in the control village are largely the game of the village elite, who only recently split into two factions. As compared to the Project village, not much happens in the control village's political arena. With regard to the everyday interactions between the poor and other villagers we observed a higher level of articulation and self-confidence in the Project village. In both villages labour conditions largely remained the same. This is primarily due to lack of increase of bargaining power in this field, which is related to the macro-economic condition of an abundance of migrant labourers.

The position of the women

The study's result concerning effects on the position of women was blurred by the influence of religion. Still, some effects seemed to be clear.

Women participating in Project activities were considerably more often involved in taking outside loans than other women. The regularity and continuity of their borrowing from BRDB was related to their organizational strength which came from membership in the same Project group. They also appeared to have a bigger say than other poor women in the taking and spending of their own loans and those of their husbands. Though the women themselves thought differently, we found little influence of all poor women on decision-making regarding marriages. Their major say still concerns the marriage of a daughter, like it used to be. Girls still generally are not allowed to vent their view of their future husband.

There did not seem to be any significant change in customs of women taking food, but here the religious factor had much influence.

Divorces had low prevalence among the Muslim poor and the majority of Muslim women were not afraid of being divorced. Quarrels between men and women occur regularly, but we did not hear of any case of wife beating.

Between the two villages there was a marked difference with regard to women's freedom to move around. These differences are partly connected with religious differences. Hindu women seemingly less easily gaining more mobility. This is contrary to their higher level of education. Among the Muslim women the Project participants were most mobile, but difference was less than could have been expected. In other words, other poor Muslim women did benefit from their example. Poor women in the Project village, and especially the poor Muslim women, have a larger share in outdoor economic activities than used to be the case. The price of their increased mobility is a heavier work burden.

The women who joined the Project have become more radical in their behaviour. They supported the men in the *khas* land dispute and played a prominent role during election times.

Organization and unity of the poor

Poor women in the project village still form a relatively cohesive collective, with exceptionally strong leadership. Their present activities are less than before and concentrate on borrowing money, health education and their food security fund. The incidence of meetings is reduced.

The male Project group, once very strong, has become defunct. It has disintegrated as a consequence of the negative results of their collective actions.

Both economic and political actions led to high levels of participation and groupness when going well. But the overall risks and costs of such endeavour are high. It also appears to be very difficult to take off again after a sequence failures.

An important and, may be, crucial achievement is the development of a supra-village organization of the Project groups. Finally we found that in each village a viable male credit fund had sprung up spontaneously.

The worldview of the poor

In the introductory chapter two contrasting idealtypes of world views of the poor were formulated : the survival model and the emancipation model. During the study we used their composing elements as beacons when probing about poor respondents' views about their present and their future. Both the models being theoretical constructs, their main value is in aiding a research operation.

When considering our findings on the worldview of the poor, we further have to take into account that our study, even though it took several months of fieldwork, only registered the poors' views at a certain stretch of time. People's views are moulded by their experiences, and their worldview will change according to recent mishaps or windfalls which occurred in their lives. In other words, the picture we present is only one set of interpretations out of a continuous sequence which may go through sudden and slow changes.

A final introductory remark to be made here is that people's interpretation of reality are usually neither very clear-cut, nor overall consistent. Their views may be diffuse and incorporate elements which were contrasted in the theoretical constructions we set out from.

In Sunamganj especially among the women participating in the Project group, borrowing money from BRDB and getting some income by working outside their homes, we found strong indications of a tendency to strive for economic betterment. Among others, like the participants in a private credit fund, such indications might be there, but they were less clearly marked. Among the men previously organized by the Project we sensed a relapse from aspirations they had harboured before.

As to the foundations of poverty, we found in all samples a low level of conviction that fate, *karma* or the will of God were responsible for general or individual poverty. On the other hand, people often mentioned plain economic causes, like "shortage of land" and "unavailability of inputs", as well as disasters and other burdens, as causes of poverty. This might, of course, also be interpreted as indicative of feelings of of powerlessness to change one's conditions.

The conviction that political-economic factors, such as unequal distribution of land, caused poverty was held by many. However, the interpretation of interview data is not so easy here. A clear-cut conclusion that those who participated in the Project are more outspoken in this respect can certainly not be drawn.

Another observation to be made is the prevalence of self-accusation in people's worldview. In all samples a considerable number of respondents defined the background of their poverty in terms of their own short comings like "lack of tenacity" or "large family size". In fact, here is a factor for which our two models do not account.

Not susprisingly, given the above statement, there was

also a clear tendency in all three samples to emphasise changes in one's own orientation or behaviour, e. g. "work harder" or "have a smaller family" as the road to improved conditions. This inclination was found in all samples.

Support from external sources, especially the government and the political parties, was found to have been largely lacking in the eyes of the poor. They clearly felt isolated in this respect, though some of them acknowledged the assistance of the NGDO responsible for initiation of the Project. Many poor people thought the government should do more for them ; such feelings did not exist with regard to political parties. We found neither confidence nor expectations towards them.

As to the confidence of people to change their situation by their own actions, the following remarks can be made. First, such confidence was highest among the female Project-group members. Second, when it was expressed by people in general they usually pointed at the need to change themselves, e. g. by holding the view that the poor's conditions will improve when they work harder. Third, emphasis on political-economic changes, which we found both in the Project sample and in one of the control samples may be interpreted in this way. Fourth, many of the poor showed confidence of their future to improve, but mentioned different ways for this to happen.

Among all the poor, their household, village, *samaj* and relatives are principal points of reference, with the exception of the female Project group members. In their case the group has gained equal importance. This used to be the same among the men, but not any more.

There have been and still are traces of solidarity with the poor outside the village among the men, and nowadays especially among the women, who joined the Project-groups. This supra-village element, which is nowadays also reflected in the regional landless association (the Secretariat), must be considered as a great achievement, considering how atomized the poor who have not been organized still are.

Finally, except for the women in the Project group, and may be also the men forming the private credit societies, cooperation between the poor is not considered a major path to improvement of socio-economic conditions. There certainly is cooperation and mutuality to a certain extent, but this is primarily looked upon as a way to help each other to survive.

The Emphasis on Credit Approach

The economic aspect

In Tangail we found that the poor of the Bank village had been more upwardly mobile than those in the control village. Participants in Bank activities showed most upward mobility. Changes in economic position occur suddenly and swiftly; downward mobility is also common. The changes in economic position of the poor in the Bank village have been the consequence of a combination of interventions by the Bank and a general economic improvement in the wake of agricultural modernization which boosted petty trading.

Access to cheap and sizeable credit has been of major importance to the poor, as it enabled them to either change their earning from wage labour to trading, or afforded them to finance an additional source of income.

In the control village the impact of agricultural modernization has been similar, but a restrictive cultural code and lack of cheap credit sources stood in the way of the poor improving themselves economically.

Local wage labourers' bargaining power did not increase, due to abundance of migrant labourers. Money lending is still important for the poor of both villages. The poor of the control village use traditional sources. Those of the Bank village nowadays get less credit from traditional *mahajans* in the village. Instead they go to wholesalers in a nearby town or borrow from small-scale money lenders who belong to their own economic category. Among these women figure prominently. Credit from moneylenders is primarily used to cover disaster spending and pay off other loans. The Bank's activities do not really offer a comparable solution to disaster spending.

The political situation in the village

In both villages politics are factional in character. Still, in the Bank village patron-client ties have weakened considerably as the poor are less dependent on internal resources. They are not, however, independent, as is shown by efforts of some of them to get land on a sharecropping basis. Such efforts are often thwarted because landowners increasingly prefer to have their land tilled by wage labourers. This development could not be observed in the control village. In both villages the quality and quantity of meals supplied to wage labourers was reported to have declined.

Interaction between poor and well-to-do peasants in the Bank village has decreased ; in the control village no difference was reported. The disparity between Bank and control village is marked. The behaviour of the poor in the control village towards the elite is one of deference ; in the Bank village it is a mixture of deference and disregard. In both villages the poor spoke extremely negative about the elite of their respective village.

Examples of collective or individual resistance of the poor are rare in both the villages. Those we came across were usually attempts to redress a wrong, which upset conditions considered to be just by the poor.

The poor have voted in line with faction or *samaj* alignments. They have not used an opportunity to vote for a representative from their own class which was available in 1983.

The position of the women

In both the villages poor women bring in an income. In the control village they work as housemaid and are paid in kind. In the Bank village poor women are engaged in trading or moneylending or may work in the local ricemill. In the last case they are paid in kind.

A considerable number of women in the Bank village have acquired a little leeway with regard to the spending of their earnings or the taking of loans.

We did not find any positive change in their control on how their husbands spend their income. In the control village things have not changed and are markedly different from those in the Bank village. Women's influence on the marriage of their children has not increased, though there is marked dissimilarity between the villages in this respect.

There is a striking disparity between the villages with regard to the education of poor girls : in the Bank village they are encouraged to go to primary school, in the control village to go to the religious school.

There did not seem to be much improvement in poor women's position in terms of the general treatment (food, beating, abusing, divorce).

The mobility of poor women in the Bank village has increased considerably. This development is directly related to the interventions of the Bank. The change applies to both women who have engaged in Bank activities and others. In this respect the effect of interventions have gone beyond the immediate participants.

The organization of the poor

The groups which were organized by the Bank, are the only organizational platform of the Bank village. In the control village there are two private credit funds,

Besides, some poor women there have formed nuclei of groups because they are eager to have the Bank come to their village. Those who borrow from the Bank see it mainly as an additional source of credit. Their major commitment is to their own households' economic improvement. There have been various collective economic actions in the Bank village. They have not been successful and the zest to participate in them has clearly diminished among the men. There is some small scale mutuality among the poor, as in supporting each other in case of improving a house, but its level did not seem to have increased.

All the poor in both villages were extremely negative about the possibility of unity among them, of united action which could be successful, and of strong leadership emerging from among them.

The worldview of the poor

When comparing our findings regarding the worldview of the poor with the two models we distinguished earlier, the same general remarks apply as were formulated in the comparative section on Sunamganj.

In Tangail we found a strong tendency to strive for improvement, especially among men and women participating the Bank activities. Though much preoccupied with how to improve their situation, the poor's vulnerability was still such that all of them had to continuously consider their survival as well. General and individual poverty were largely attributed to individual shortcomings characteristic of the poor, or to plain economic causes. Actions of others or political-economic changes were not considered essential to improvement of conditions to the same extent, though women from all three samples attached more importance to it than the men did. Though there were differences among the poor, most of them, especially men and women in the control village, were positive about government support received in the past. Support from political parties was neither acknowledged, nor expected. There was a clear disparity between the villages as to the importance of primordial ties as main reference points for one's behaviour. In the control village such ties were extremely strong and village society put clear limits to people's behaviour, most restrictively so in the case of women. In the Bank village horizontal mobility had increased among both men and women. Poor people had found new reference points in their Bank-group and among colleague traders in the *bazaar*. Patron-client ties had clearly weakened in the Bank village, due to both macro economic causes and the intervention by the Bank, but still were strong in the control village.

In the control village poor people only cooperate with other poor in the context of primordial settings and in the two recent credit funds. In the Bank village poor people cooperate with other poor in the Bank groups and in collective economic actions. Moreover, they have ties with the poor of other villages in meetings and workshops organized by the Bank.

All the poor have low expectations of the feasibility of cooperation among themselves. Their negative views of themselves in this respect were really striking.

2. Reflections

In the preceeding pages we have described how, in their own way, each of the two development approaches has been in general terms quite effective. Next, we shall reflect on some of the findings from the position of critical onlookers, with the intention to make some positive remarks on selected issues. If we consider it helpful, we shall refer to observations made by others with regard to similar situations. These final observations have to be brief and we hope they will stimulate others to look further into the problems we can only touch.

Size of groups and their organization

Both the Project and the Bank chose the group as the medium for supporting the poor, though with a different emphasis. As the Project stresses collective action as a main road to alleviating poverty, the groups have become the backbone of the poor's development activities. This is, of course, already a further phase in the development process. At an earlier stage the groups was used for promotion of awareness building and further growth of feelings of a common identity. Though there are some individual provisions, like the food security fund, these exist only on the assumption that the group is a viable concern. If the group collapses, like the male group did, individual drawing rights disappear as well. The group is also the building element for the supra-village organization of the poor. So, in various ways, a viable group is at the heart of this development approach.

In Tangail the groups have another position. They are, foremost, the vehicle the Bank needs to reach the individual poor and to change and control his behaviour. In addition, the group is supposed to provide the individual with some economic security, though this did not seem to amount to much in the situation we studied. Further, the groups provide a means to organize collective action, but this is not, as in Sunamganj, a primary concern.

There is no doubt that group formation is the only way to go ahead for both the development approaches. Still, it is a road with pitfalls. As to the situation in Sunamganj, we observed four major issues in this respect. One is the maintenance of the balance between what individual members put in over the years and what they do get out of it. Most of the results attained are collective and indivisible, like the improvement in the position of women. Everybody shares in them, but that does not imply that everybody will deem sufficient in terms of the personal efforts put in or losses incurred. Possibly, a form of individual support may serve as a kind of shock-absorber in the relation between group and individual. On the other hand, such an element creates difficulties of its own, and it is not certain whether these or the advantages will supersede at the level of the whole group.

Second, there is the mobilization problem. Human collectives gain strength only through common activities. After the initial period of group formation a situation had been reached where the groups were only mobilized intermittently, apart from some on going activities in the women's group. Still, for collective feelings to survive it is absolutely necessary that there are sufficient occasions for the expectations which the members have of each other to be positively confirmed. In our view here lies part of the explanation of the ultimate demise of the Jaipur male group.

Third, there is the matter of group size. Here the Project's approach faces a dilemma. For its major strategy of collective action a large number of organized poor is required, which would make large groups essential. Still, as group theory taught us long ago (Olson, 1965 ; 43-48), large groups (or conglomerates of many small ones) face more organizational costs and and problems than small ones and contain more internal tensions to break down.

Fourth, the supra-village organization which is presently growing and gathering strength in the long run may face some severe difficulties. Here, again, a balance must be struck between the contribuant, costs and benefits, though now there are two layers of contribuants, groups and individual members, which have to be appeased. In this respect it may be instructive to look at early unionism in the West, which, essentially, had to deal with the same problem. There it was solved partly by introducing some individual benefits, such as fair price shops and legal advice (Olson, 1981, chapter III). Such lessons may be translated to the Bangladesh situation in terms of the first point we raised, i.e., finding some form of individual benefit. Further by stressing the need for strong groups covering most poor villagers as a precondition for a viable organization. First things should come first : strong groups must be maintained or the higher level organization will be doomed. The above points do not appear to equally apply to the situation in Bank villages in Tangail, where groups are small and individual benefits, in terms of getting loans, are rather clear. Still, when we take a closer look, a few issues may be raised here as well. Problems with groups will arise particularly in larger collectives and over longer time spans. As to the Bank-groups this implies that problems will most easily crop up at the *kendra* or village-level, the more so, because this is the level where collective economic actions are initiated, which, as we shall see below, generate their own difficulties. Besides, we have to stress here that the Bank village we studied was a small one ; for getting insight in the queries at hand, a bigger village would be more appropriate. Further, the chance that organizational problems occur appears to increase with passing of time, because individually successful members' interest in groups and groups' activities may wane.

As yet, the collective element of the Bank's activities has been limited to economic actions, meetings, workshops and seminars. Demonstrations and confrontations are no part of this development approach. Still, to the extent that collective action is valued, the need to develop and sustain a culture of collectiveness has to be taken care of. This is the more important-and difficult for that matter-as we have found a high prevalence of individualist and competitive notions among the poor. In so far as the Bank emphasizes individual economic improvement, such notions may presently be stimulated.

Economic and other collective actions

In both study areas examples of collective actions were found. We have to distinguish between collective actions aiming at direct improvement of economic conditions, and those which aim at changes in the access to resources or to positions pivotal to such access. To all the collective actions applies that the level of groupness, of collectiveness, increases in the course of them. Besides, the participants' interpretations of reality may change considerably, depending on the outcome (Scott, 1985 ; 345).

Collective economic actions were found especially, though not exclusively, in Tangail, and we described some of them in Chapter III. The ventures of the male groups either ended in failure or only just earned the benefit of the doubt (the powertiller). Two observations may be made, namely why there is a high prevalence of (imminent) failures and how to estimate the damage done and the future possiblities. Reasons for failure have been climatic disasters, lack of management skills in combination with the detachment necessary for running this kind of economic operation, mismatchment between the necessary time frame of the economic venture (medium term) and that of the poor men involved in it (short term). The short term perspective of the poor is also evident in their borrowing behaviour and trading ventures, and is well suited for a situation characterized by insecurity.

Obviously, the first factor—climatic calamities— can only be eliminated by selecting ventures outside agriculture. The second set of factors are only partly a matter of time and training. The other part concerns the question whether professional management and financial administration would be a better choice. It also would solve the problem of detachment, as an outsider would not have to face the many and often conflicting claims on money, work, delay of contribution, that a villager will always be facing.

The consequences of a failing collective economic venture may be dire indeed, the more so if they form a sequence. On the one hand there are the losses, to be borne by the members, who see them as one more disaster which has hurt them. On the other hand there is the price in terms of breakdown of feelings of mutual trust, of disappearance of an embryonic belief in the feasibility of collective ventures, of rifts in the group and, last but not least, of diminishing confidence in the Bank. Such effects may ripple for a long time, whence it appears advisable to not only consider each new venture very carefully, but, possibly, reconsider the viability and value of the strategy as such.

The other kind of collective action, focussing at the poor's access to resources, could be found primarily in Sunamganj. This kind of collective behaviour has been the subject of many good studies of poor peasants' resistance, like Scott

(1985). Before making one more distinction, we want to stress that each of these actions has a specific characteristic, which may put a heavy strain on it (Olson, 1965 ; de Swaan, 1984). The crux is that a real collective good is undividable (implying that the economic ventures just discussed are in this particular sense no collective actions). Nobody can be excluded from the benefit (e.g. access to *khas* land), whether he has really contributed or not, and, if the number of contribuants is high enough, some one's lesser contribution may even have no observable effect on the final outcome. Obviously this puts a heavy burden on the mutual trust and also may lead to participants not doing their utmost, as nobody may observe this anyhow. It also seems to be applicable specially in a cultural environment where individualist and competitive notions are rife, as seemed for instance to be the case among the poor in Tangail.

If we look at the Sunamganj cases of collective action concerning the access the poor have to resources and to positions crucial to that, we can easily distinguish one kind which aims at redressing a wrong. In fact, what happens is that a prevailing condition in, for instance, labour relations is broken by "the other side", followed by an action of the poor with the objective to undo this perceived injustice. They do not want to change their world, but want to keep what they consider their legitimate right.

The other kind of collective action is intended to change the world, with the *khas* land case and the elections as prime examples. In both these cases, by the way, the Project has been the initiator, contrary to the cases of redress we mentioned just before. Moreover, in both cases the poor only exercise rights which the law has granted them.

Looking more closely at the *khas* land and election cases it strikes one that the costs and traumas of the *khas* land dispute have been considerable and some of our previous remarks on the aftermath of economic actions are applicable here as well. The second observation is that it is very hard indeed to find issues which open a way to a better life for the poor and, at the same time, have the necessary mobilization value. The struggle for access to *khas* land was tough and unsuccessful and if won, it would have remained a bone of contention between the poor and their adversaries for some time to come. But it is not easy to see an issue with the same potential and value (land) attached to it. Elections have another problem. If *khas* land is always available in each village, elections are timed by the state and may be fixed and unfixed at a whim. There are few and the outcome is unreliable. An additional problem is that voting for representation at higher administrative levels is less of an immediate concern for the poor. As both Scott (1985) and Piven and Cloward (1977) stress, the poor will get mobilized soonest for subjects they relate to directly, like the local moneylender or U.P. member.

What it all boils down to is that in the future probably still some hard thinking must be done on opening new venues for this kind of collective actions. In

Sunamganj this heavy task has now become that of the Secretariat and the groups it represents. Their success will be of utmost importance to others involved in the same struggle for improvement elsewhere in Bangladesh.

The Way Ahead

It is not our intention to provide policy directions and the study was not designed to lead to them. Still, there are some clues which may be of direct relevance to policy makers. Both the development approaches did result in positive effects for the target-group. Yet, in both cases there are, as was shown in the previous pages, some pertinent questions about future perspectives. We shall not repeat them again.

Next, there are some more general lessons to be learned. First, the poor feel isolated and there can be no question about the importance of the role of NGDOs and union-like organization in acting as go-betweens and connecting the poor villagers of a region. Second, the poor are quite well able to maintain their own supra-level organization to a certain extent, but due to their poverty such organization may need outside support for some time to come. Assistance, however, should not be understood as interference. Third, in borth areas there appeared to be scope for the poor to engage in improving their living environment. The Bank has already taken an initiative by providing loans for housing, to be made available in Konabari shortly. Other schemes of such a nature are to be recommended, certainly also in an area like Sunamganj, where, despite many non-material improvements, amelioration of the quality of material life has lagged behind. Emphasis on conscientization, in other words, does not necessarily have to imply that other support has to be kept out at all costs. To us it seems a matter of emphasis. Fourth and final the poor's expectations of government support appear to be unrealistic at present. Still among them there are those who recognize and emphasize the government's duty in this respect.

Table : 2.2 Main sources of income of heads of households in Jaipur-West and Nayagram

Source	Jaipur-West		Nayagram	
	Number	Percentage	Number	Percentage
Cultivation	62	35.6	68	63.6
Wage labour	56	32.2	26	24.3
Trading	15	8.6	3	2.8
Dependent	13	7.4	6	5.6
Fishing	11	6.3	—	—
Artisan	5	2.9	—	—
House work for others	5	2.9	3	2.8
Service	4	2.3	1	.9
Beggar	1	.6	—	—
Brokerage	1	.6	—	—
Barber	1	.6	—	—
Total	174	100.0	107	100.0

Source : Census November-December 1985.

Table : 2.3 Mains source of income now and eight years ago of heads of sample households in Sunamgonj

Main sources of income	S_1				S_2				S_3			
	A		B		A		B		A		B	
	Now	Then	Now	Then	Now	Ther	Now	Then	Now	Then	Now	Then
Cultivation	5	8	2	2	5	9	2	4	8	9	10	10
Wage labour	12	15	—	—	10	11	—	—	7	7	—	—
Trade	3	2	—	—	4	1	1	—	1	—	—	—
Others	5	—	2	2	6	4	1	—	1	1	—	—
Total	25	25	4	4	25	25	4	4	17	17	10	10

Source : Interviews with heads of sample households.

Table : 2.4 Views of heads of sample households in Sunamgonj. Comparing present and past economic situation (8 years back).

View of present economic condition	S_1	S_2	S_3
Better	11	16	14
Same	16	8	10
Worse	2	5	3
Total	29	29	27

Source : Interviews with heads of sample households.

Table : 2.5 Prevalence and main sources of outside income of adult poor women

	Jaipur-West				Nayagram			
	A	B	Total		A	B	Total	
			No	%			No	%
Total no. of adult women	213	49	262	100.0	84	47	131	100.0
No. of women earning	32	3	35	13.4	11	5	16	12.2
Trading*1	16	1	17	6.5	—	—	—	—
House work for others	11	—	11	4.2	6	—	6	4.6
Cultivation*2	5	1	6	2.3	5	5	10	7.6
Service	—	1	1	.4	—	—	—	—

Source : Census November-December 1985.

* Trading includes : Paddy husking, kitchen gardening, poultry-keeping, dairy, hawking.

* The earners mentioned here are all widows and heads of their respective households.

Table : 2.6 Distribution of landownership of households in Jaipur-West and Nayagram

Holding size (in Decimals)	Jaipur-West		Nayagram	
	Number	Percentage	Number	Percentage
No land	79	45.4	25	23.4
1-10	—	—	—	—
10-50	15	8.6	4	3.7
50-100	21	12.1	9	8.4
100-200	35	20.1	31	29.0
200-500	14	8.0	16	15.0
500-1000	4	2.3	10	9.3
1000-5000	6	3.5	12	11.2
Total	174	100.0	107	100.0

Source : Census November-December 1985.

Table : 2.7 Membership of poor adult women in Jaipur-West and Jaipur-East in project groups.

Village	Total number of poor women over 15 years	Membership	
		Number	Percentage
Jaipur-West	262	61	23.3
Jaipur-East	346	62	17.9
Total	608	123	20.2

Source : Census November-December 1985.

Table : 2.8 Views of heads of poor households and adult women regarding roots of general poverty.*

Sl No	Na'ure of causes	S_1			S_2			S_3		
		Male	Female	Total	Male	Female	Total	Male	Female	Total
I	Day to day/ Sudden disasters and other burdens	2	1	3	5	3	8	1	6	7
II	Will of God/ *Karma*/Fate	2	3	5	2	2	4	—	1	1
III	Plain Economic	2	10	12	1	3	4	13	15	28
IV	Political-Economic	8	10	18	3	6	9	10	13	23
V	Self-Accusation	6	2	8	1	4	5	3	1	4
VI	No Opinion	11	10	21	—	2	2	—	—	—

Source : Interviews of members of sample households.

*Joint figures for economic categories A and B.

Table : 2.10 Views of heads of poor households and adult women regarding solutions for general poverty.*

Sl No.	Nature of Solution	S_1			S_2			S_3		
		Male	Female	Total	Male	Female	Total	Male	Female	Total
I	God's will/ *Karma*/Fate	3	3	6	7	8	15	—	—	—
II	Government Action	5	9	14	2	4	6	3	11	14
III	Self Change	6	12	18	10	12	22	10	7	17
IV	Plain Economic Change	4	2	6	4	7	11	5	4	9
V	Political-economic Change	6	13	19	1	1	2	12	3	15
VI	Despair	2	—	2	—	—	—	—	—	—
VII	No Opinion	3	4	7	—	—	—	3	8	11

Source : interviews of members of sample households.

*Joint figures for economic categories A and B.

Table : 2.9 Views of heads of poor households and adult women regarding causes of their own poverty.*

Sl No	Nature of causes	S_1			S_2			S_3		
		Male	Female	Total	Male	Female	Total	Male	Female	Total
I	Day to day/sudden disasters and other burdens	10	11	21	13	10	23	10	14	24
II	Will of God/ *Karma*/Fate	2	2	4	2	2	4	—	1	1
III	Plain Economic	10	25	35	17	18	35	21	19	40
IV	Political-Economic	6	11	17	5	10	15	6	6	12
V	Self-Accusation	6	5	11	5	7	12	10	5	15
VI	No Opinion	—	2	2	—	2	2	—	—	—

Source : Interviews of members of sample households.
*Joint figures for economic categories A and B.

Table : 2.11 Views of heads of poor households and adult women regarding solutions for their individual poverty.*

Sl No.	Nature of Solution	S_1			S_2			S_3		
		Male	Female	Total	Male	Female	Total	Male	Female	Total
I	God's will/ *Karma*/Fate	3	3	6	6	8	14	—	1	1
II	Government Action	3	7	10	6	5	11	4	11	15
III	Self Change	6	11	17	12	10	22	10	8	18
IV	Plain-Economic Change	4	3	7	12	5	17	6	3	9
V	Political-Economic Change	4	8	12	1	1	2	10	3	13
VI	Despair	—	1	1	1	1	2	—	2	2
VII	No Opinion	3	3	6	1	5	6	—	—	—

Source : Interviews of members of sample households.

*Joint figures for economic categories A and B.

Table : 3.2 Main source of income of heads of households in Konabari and Radhapur.

Source of income	Konabari		Radhapur	
	No.	%	No.	%
Wage labour	7	9.7	16	13.0
Cultivation	25	34.7	47	38.2
Trade	31	43.1	21	17.1
Service	2	2.8	3	2.4
Artisan	2	2.8	—	—
Rickshaw driver	2	2.8	4	3.3
Shop-keeper	1	1.4	2	1.6
House work for others	1	1.4	4	3.3
Fishing	—	—	9	7.3
Dependents	1	1.4	10	8.1
Begging	—	—	6	4.9
Horse cart driver	—	—	1	0.8
Total	72	100.1	123	100.0

Source : Census November-December 1985.

Table : 3.2 Main source of income of heads of households in Konabari and Radhapur.

Source of income	Konabari		Radhapur	
	No.	%	No.	%
Wage labour	7	9.7	16	13.0
Cultivation	25	34.7	47	38.2
Trade	31	43.1	21	17.1
Service	2	2.8	3	2.4
Artisan	2	2.8	—	—
Rickshaw driver	2	2.8	4	3.3
Shop-keeper	1	1.4	2	1.6
House work for others	1	1.4	4	3.3
Fishing	—	—	9	7.3
Dependents	1	1.4	10	8.1
Begging	—	—	6	4.9
Horse cart driver	—	—	1	0.8
Total	72	100.1	123	100.0

Source : Census November-December 1985.

Table : 3.3 Main sources of income of heads of poor sample households.*

Source of income	Konabari		Radhapur	
	No.	%	No.	%
Wage labour	7	12.7	19	21.8
Cultivation	13	23.7	25	28.7
Trade	28	50.9	71	19.6
Others	7	12.7	26	29.9
Total	55	100.0	87	100.0

Source : Census November-December 1985.

*Poor households include economic categories A and B.

Table : 3.4 Main sources of income now and five years ago of heads of sample households.

Source income	T_1				T_2				T_3			
	A		B		A		B		A		B	
	Now	Then	Now	Then	Now	Then	Now	Then	Now	Then	Now	Then
Wage labour	3	6	1	4	4	4	4	4	8	6	1	3
Cultivation	—	—	4	3	1	1	2	1	1	2	6	5
Trade	7	5	9	7	3	4	5	3	1	2	2	1
Others	1	—	—	—	1	—	1	1	2	2	1	1
Total	11	11	14	14	9	9	9	9	12	12	10	10

Source : Interviews with heads of sample households.

Table : 3.5 Views of poor* sample households comparing present and past economic situation (5 years ago).

View of present economic situation	T_1	T_2	T_3
Better	19	9	7
Same	2	5	14
Worse	4	4	1
Total	25	18	22

Source : Interviews with heads of sample household
*Poor include category A and B households.

Table : 3.6 Distribution of landownership of households in Konabari and Radhapur

Size in Decimals	Konabari		Radhapur	
	No	%	No	%
No land	34	47.2	48	39.1
1-10	2	2.8	6	4.9
10-50	15	20.8	25	20.3
50-100	6	8.3	18	14.6
100-200	5	6.9	11	8.9
200-500	5	6.9	10	8.1
500-1000	5	6.9	4	3.2
1000-5000	—	—	1	0.8
Total	72	99.8	123	99.9

Source : Census November-December 1985.

Table : 3.7 Membership of Bank-group of heads of households in Konabari

Economic category	Total no. of household	Membership of Bank-group	
		No.	%
A	20	10	50.0
B	35	25	71.4
C	12	4	33.3
D	5	—	—
Total	72	39	54.2

Source : Census November-December 1985.

Table 3.8 Membership of Bank-groups of adult women in Konabari

Economic category	Total no. of adult women	Membership of group	
		No	%
A	24	2	8.3
B	51	17	33·3
C	24	2	8.3
D	12	—	—
Total	111	21	18.9

Source : Census November-December 1985,

Table : 3.9 Prevalence and main sources of outside income of adult poor women

	Konabari				Radhapur			
	A	B	Total		A	B	Total	
			No	%			No	%
Total no. of adult women	24	51	75	100	49	44	93	100.0
No. of women earning	17	24	41	54.7	10	10	20	21.5
Trading*	13	21	34	45.3	4	9	13	14.0
House work for others	1	1	2	2.7	5	1	6	6.5
Cultivation	—	1	1	1.3	—	—	—	—
Wage labour	3	1	4	5.3	—	—	—	—
Teaching	—	—	—	—	1	—	1	1.1

Source : Census November-December 1985.

* Trading includes : Paddy husking, kitchen gardening, poultry-keeping, muri processing, sale of trees, dairy,

Note : Money-lending as female source of income was only mentioned in the in-depth interviews

Table : 3.10 Views of heads of poor households and adult women regarding roots of general poverty.*

Sl No.	Nature of causes	T_1			T_2			T_3		
		Male	Female	Total	Male	Female	Total	Male	Female	Total
I	Day to day/sudden disasters and other burdens	—	4	4	3	1	4	—	2	2
II	Will of God/ *Karma*/Fate	3	2	5	3	5	8	3	4	7
III	Plain Economic	17	21	38	11	13	24	17	26	43
IV	Political-Economic	2	6	8	—	2	2	2	4	6
V	Self-Accusation	4	14	18	12	5	17	4	12	16
VI	No Opinion	6	4	10	—	6	6	6	1	7

Source : Interviews of members of sample households.
*Joint figures for economic categories A and B.

Table : 3.11 Views of heads of poor households and adult women regarding causes of their own poverty.*

Sl No	Nature of causes	T_1			T_2			T_3		
		Male	Female	Total	Male	Female	Total	Male	Female	Total
I	Day to day/ Sudden disasters and other burdens	12	10	22	2	—	2	6	3	9
II	Will of God/ *Karma*/Fate	2	2	4	4	5	9	5	12	17
III	Plain Economic	21	25	46	10	18	28	18	27	45
IV	Political-Economic	2	11	13	—	5	5	3	—	3
V	Self-Accusation	13	8	21	8	11	19	7	13	20
VI	No Opinion	2	3	5	—	1	1	2	2	4

Source : Interviews of members of sample households.

*Joint figures for economic categories A and B.

Table : 3.12 Views of heads of poor households and adult women regarding solutions for general poverty.*

Sl No.	Nature of Solution	T_1			T_2			T_3		
		Male	Female	Total	Male	Female	Total	Male	Female	Total
I	God's will/ *Karma*/Fate	6	3	9	2	6	8	8	7	15
II	Government Action	3	3	6	1	—	1	1	—	1
III	Self Change	12	11	23	10	14	24	1	13	14
IV	Plain Economic Change	6	11	17	3	10	13	—	16	16
V	Political-economic Change	4	14	18	2	5	7	2	7	9
VI	Despair	2	1	3	—	—	—	1	—	1
VII	No Opinion	6	5	11	2	4	6	10	6	16

Source : Interviews of members of sample households.

*Joint figures for economic categories A and B.

Table : 3.13 Views of heads of poor households and adult women regarding solutions for their individual poverty.*

Sl No.	Nature of Solution	T_1			T_2			T_3		
		Male	Female	Total	Male	Female	Total	Male	Female	Total
I	God's will/ *Karma*/Fate	6	4	10	3	5	8	13	5	18
II	Government Action	3	3	6	1	1	2	—	—	—
III	Self-Change	12	13	25	13	13	26	5	15	20
IV	Plain Economic Change	10	13	23	3	11	14	2	17	19
V	Political-Economic Change	5	15	20	2	5	7	3	7	10
VI	Despair	2	1	3	—	—	—	—	—	—
VII	No Opinion	4	3	7	1	2	3	3	2	5

Source : Interviews of members of sample households.

***Joint figures for economic categories A and B.**

Annexure-II

Methodological Note

As it is important for readers to be able to gauge the value of the material presented and of the conclusions based on it some methodological problems will be mentioned briefly.

1. Each of the two projects representing a specific development approach was carefully selected, particularly because they combined a long intervention period with clear predominance of a specific approach. Still, in both cases we also found traces of the other approach, e. g. in Sunamganj there was provision of credit till 1981 and in Tangail awareness raising about other matters than loans began in 1985. Here we see a clear example of the fact that society is not a laboratory and that in case of longitudinal studies we can only try to proceed under the best conditions available.

2. Even though the researchers spent about half a year in the villages this was not enough to establish the level of confidentiality necessary for getting sufficiently reliable information on matters the poor do not easily discuss with outsiders, especially

moneylending. Moreover, the research time in the field was insufficient for a proper budget study. In fact, the study has been a mixture of a survey and an anthropological in-depth study, including most of the strengths but also some of the weaknesses of both.

3. It was not easy to realize the study in the way it was designed, because in both cases the coverage of the project concerned was so high that very few control villages were left. Especially in Tangail our choice was extremely limited, so that we ended up with Radhapur, which was culturally rather dissimilar to neighbouring villages. Nevertheless, the study of Radhapur has deepened our insight and we could, fortunately, support the control element with an additional control sample from Konabari itself.

4. The study focussed on the rural poor and was limited to four villages. This implies that the effects of the interventions on the rural local elite and on the regional power structure were not studied in much depth.

5. In both locations the researchers did not actually reside in the villages themselves, but at a few kilometers' distance. This situation had both advantages and disadvantages. A relatively quiet residence elsewhere allowed the researchers to regularly discuss their interviews and observations, as well as any frustrating event that might have

happened. Still, not spending most evenings in the villages implied missing an opportunity to collect information and observe daily affairs.

6. The mixed composition of the sub-teams worked out extremely well in Sunamganj with its Hindu majority population. The main impediment to conducting interviews there, was that the Muslim female researcher was usually not allowed to enter houses of Hindus. In Tangail, however, the female researcher met a lot of objections among especially the women of the control village. The women objected against her moving around comparatively freely and to her working together with a man. Though she tried to work inconspicuously, she had, in fact, a hard time in this village. Things would probably have been easier if in this particular case the fieldteam would have consisted of two women and one man. In Konabari initially the sub-team was not received warmly, but this changed drastically when the researchers–the female researcher was a trained nurse–was able to offer some medical assistance in case of an emergency. In spite of the difficulties encountered in the control village, we still feel strongly about the necessity of fielding female researchers when conducting studies like the present one. It is, therefore, fortunate that the number of women experienced in this difficult line of work appears to be increasing in Bangladesh.

7. In both locations the researchers were initially identified with the project organization. During the census they did, however, explain their position over and over again. Eventually, in the course of their stay the level of identification reduced drastically.

8. In Tangail the collection of information was hampered by the harvest, when for some time it was difficult to interview the men ; in Sunamganj there was no harvest this year due to the bad weather.

Glossary

Aman	:	Autumn (late summer) rice
Aus	:	Early summer rice
Bil	:	Extremely low lying area
Borga	:	Sharecropping
Borgadar	:	Sharecropper
Boro	:	Winter rice
BRDB	:	Bangladesh Rural Development Board
Chan	:	Supra village subcaste council
Chor	:	Thief
Dheki	:	A wooden instrument to husk paddy
Eid	:	Muslim religious festival held twice a year
Gonokendra	:	People's Centre
Gram Sarker	:	Now defunct village government introduced by late president Ziaur Rahman in 1980
Gusti	:	Patrilineage
Haat	:	Weekly/biweekly market
Haor	:	Semi-permanent lake
Imam	:	A Person who leads the Muslim prayer
Jau	:	Wheat or rice gruel
Jo	:	Prime time to carry out specific activity
Kantha	:	Quilt usually made of worn or used clothes

Karma	:	Fate
Kendra Prodhan	:	Centre-chief
Khas land	:	Government owned land
Lungi	:	Ankle length wrap worn by men
Madrasa	:	Islamic school
Mahajan	:	Traditional moneylender
Maktab	:	Islamic school for beginners
Matabar	:	Village leader
Maund	:	Measure of weight equal to 39 kg.
Moulvi	:	Learned religious man
Nagarsi	:	Drum beater
Palli	:	Rural ; village
Palli Samity	:	Privately organized credit association
Para	:	Neighbourhood
Parishad	:	Council
Piri	:	A tiny wooden plank to sit on
Pradhan	:	Chief
Puja	:	Hindu ritual
Purdah	:	Seclusion of women
Rabi crop	:	Winter crops
Rangjama	:	Yearly contract where the landowner leases out land against an advance payment in cash
Roti	:	Unleavened bread
Salish	:	Village arbitration council
Samaj	:	Village-level association
Samity	:	Association
Sari	:	Women's dress ; six yard long wrap worn around the body
Sherbet	:	Sweetened drink

Thana : Police Station ; formerly also administrative unit

Upazila : Upgraded *thana* ; important administrative unit in Bangladesh. It is headed by an elected official known as *Upazila* Chairman

Bibliography

Ahmed, M. 1980 (a), "The Savar Project: Meeting the Rural Health Crisis in Bangladesh", in *Meeting the Basic Needs of the Rural Poor*, P.H. Coombs (ed), New York

1980 (b) "BRAC: Building Human Infrastructures to Serve the Rural Poor", in *Meeting the Basic Needs of the Rural* Poor, P.H. Coombs (ed), New York

Akhter, F., Banu, S., Feldman F. 1981, *An Assessment of the Government's Health and Family Planning Programme: A Case Study of Daudkandi Thana and North Mohammadpur and Charcharua Villages in Bangladesh*, Dhaka. SIDA

Arefeen, H.K. 1986, *Changing Agrarian Structure in Bangladesh: Shimulia, A Study of a Periurban Village*, Dhaka, Centre for Social Studies

Ashraf, A. Chowdhury, S., Streefland, P. 1982 "Health, Disease and Health-care in Rural Bangladesh", in *Social Science and Medicine*, 16: 2041-2054

Blair. H.W. 1985 "Participation, Public Policy, Political Economy and Development in Rural Bangladesh, 1958-85", in *World Development*, 13 (12): 1231-1247

BRAC, 1980 *The Net: The Power Structure in Ten Villages*. Dhaka

Cain, M., 1983 "Landless in India and Bangladesh: A Critical Review of National Data Sources", in *Economic Development and Cultural Change*, 32 (1): 149-167

Chaudhury, R.H., 1981 "The Seasonality of Prices and Wages in Bangladesh", in *Seasonal Dimensions to Rural Poverty* Chambers, R. Longhurst R. and Pacey A. (eds), London

Clay, E.Z., 1981 "Seasonal Patterns of Agricultural Employment in Bangladesh", in *Seasonal Dimensions to Rural Poverty*.

Chambers, R. Longhurst R. and Pacey A. (eds), London.

Grant, J P., 1985 *The State of the Worlds Children*, New York, UNICEF.

Hartmann, B and J. Boyce, 1983, *A Quiet Violence : View from a Bangladesh Village*, London

Hassan, N. and K. Ahmad 1984 "Studies on Food and Nutrient Intake by Rural Population of Bangladesh : Comparison between Intakes of 1962-64, 1975-76 and 1981-82", in *Ecology of Food and Nutrition*, 15 (12) : 143-158

Hossain, M. Rashid, A. Jahan S. 1986 *Rural Poverty in Bangladesh : A Report to the Like-minded Group*, Dhaka Universities Research Centre.

Khan, A.R. 1977 "Poverty and Inequality in Rural Bangladesh", in *Poverty and Landlessness in South Asia*, Geneva International Labour Organization

1984 "Real Wages of Agricultural Workers in Bangladesh", in *Economic and Political Weekly*, XIX (4) : 540-48 (Review of Political Economy) :

Olson jr. M. 1965 *The Logic of Collective Action*, Massachusetts, Cambridge

Piven, F.F. and Cloward R.A., 1977 *Poor People's Movement : Why they Succeed, How they Fail*, New York

van Schendel, W. 1981 *Peasant Mobility : The Odds of Peasant Life in Bangladesh*, Assen, the Netherlands

van Schendel, W. and Faraizi, A.H. 1984 *Rural Labourers in Bengal, 1880 to 1980*, Rotterdam

Siddiqui, K. 1984 *An Evaluation of the Grameen Bank Operation*, Dhaka Grameen Bank

Sobhan, R. 1982 *The Crisis of External Dependence: The Political Economy of Foreign Aid to Bangladesh* (2nd impression), Dhaka

Scott. J. C., 1985, *Weapons of the Weak : Everyday Forms of Peasant Resistance*, New Haven.

de Swaan, A. 1984 "Workers' and Clients' Mutualism Compared : Perspectives from the Past in the Development of the Welfare State", *Paper for the Politics of the Welfare State*

Conference, Manchester, University of Manchester
de Vylder, S. 1982 *Agriculture in Chains* : *Bangladesh* : *a Case Study in Contradiction and Constraints*, London
World Bank 1985 *World Development Report*, Washington